THE ART OF DECISION-MAKING

NASHAT HELAL

PASSIONPRENEUR®
P U B L I S H I N G

THE ART OF DECISION-MAKING

Power of Choice

NASHAT HELAL

PASSIONPRENEUR®
PUBLISHING

The Art of Decision-Making
Copyright © 2024 Nashat Helal
First published in 2024

Print: 978-1-76124-160-4
E-book: 978-1-76124-161-1
Hardback: 978-1-76124-162-8

Publishing information
Publishing and design facilitated by Passionpreneur Publishing
A division of Passionpreneur Organization Pty Ltd
ABN: 48640637529

Melbourne, VIC | Australia
www.PassionpreneurPublishing.com

I dedicate this book to my hero, my late father, my source of inspiration since I was born. Through his wisdom and encouragement, he showed me the importance of empathy, kindness, and perseverance. Being a leader by example, he helped shape my character, and taught me the value of knowing myself and how to lead by example. The lessons I've learned from him have not only enriched my life, but have also created a legacy that I am proud to carry forward.

To my wife, your sacrifices, selflessness, and unending belief in my potential have shaped my path, giving me the courage to pursue my dreams and face life's challenges as they come our way. This dedication is a humble attempt to express my heartfelt appreciation for everything you've done.

To my mother, siblings, and kids, your presence, love, and acceptance have been a source of belonging and encouragement.

With all my love and gratitude.

CONTENTS

ACKNOWLEDGMENTS

I would like to acknowledge certain people who have helped me to become the person I am today in my career.

Philip Stanton
AbdulAziz Al Balushi
David Graham

I'm truly grateful for all the moments, stories, and challenges we shared and faced together. Thank you for showing me your support. Your actions and leadership have inspired me and enriched my life in more ways than I can express. Please accept my heartfelt gratitude for your trust in me and for everything you did.

Thank you once again for being such an important part of my journey.

INTRODUCTION

Every day, we are faced with choices that shape the course of our lives. Some decisions are small and not life-changing, e.g., choosing what to drink, coffee or tea, in the morning; others are more significant, altering the trajectory of our lives. The art of decision-making, a timeless and complex bridge between the mind and heart, is a skill we all must master.

In this book, we will embark on a journey into the art of decision-making. We will dive deep into the principles that underlie each choice we make, exploring the factors that influence our path. In this book, through a system of actionable tools and lessons learned, I provide guidelines to help you unlock the art and the science of decision-making so that you can make better choices.

Why is it that we often choose against our best interests? How can we unravel the complexities of our biases and emotions, which often leave us feeling lost? What can we learn from great decision-makers in history who shaped the world with their choices?

As we go through the chapters of this book, we'll uncover the principles that govern our decisions, both conscious and unconscious. We'll learn to practice the power of mindfulness to see through the cloud of uncertainty and the temptation of biases. We'll discover how to embrace uncertainty, recognizing that every choice carries within it an inherent risk.

But the art of decision-making is not just about avoiding mistakes; it's about crafting a life that aligns with our values, aspirations, and purpose. It's about harnessing the creative force within us to create new paths and seize opportunities. In the chapters that follow, we'll explore the psychology of choice, the science of decision-making, and the wisdom of those who have mastered this art.

Ultimately, 'The Art of Decision-Making' is an invitation to become not just a passive observer of life but an active participant in shaping your legacy. It's a celebration of the beautiful and sometimes messy process of decision-making, a process that defines who we are and who we can become.

So, dear reader, as we embark on this journey into the art of decision-making, let us approach each page with curiosity and open hearts, ready to embrace the choices that await us in our own lives.

CHAPTER 1

DO WE REALLY HAVE A CHOICE?

The quality of our choices determines
the quality of our lives

COWARDS DIE MANY TIMES BEFORE THEIR DEATHS;
THE VALIANT NEVER TASTE OF DEATH BUT ONCE.

— WILLIAM SHAKESPEARE, JULIUS CAESAR

When I hear this quote, like anyone else, the first thing that comes to my mind is – I would rather die one time than thousands of times.

We live a life where we make choices every single moment, every single day. We make both conscious and unconscious choices, but most fall into the latter category.

During my twenty-two years in the corporate world, I went through what most of us have either gone through or will go through, depending on your current state in your career. I truly believe that I fully understand the pain and the struggles related to our daily jobs.

I started my professional career in 2002 when I joined Ernst & Young (EY), an international firm. It is considered one of the big four firms in audit and advisory services.

Reflecting back on that moment, I wonder what would have happened if someone had handed me this book twenty years ago. What an impact it would have made on my professional life from the get-go.

For that reason, I have decided to write this book and share my relevant experiences with you; there may be someone out there who is starting their career or about to make a big choice in life who can read this book and use it as a guide.

In this book, I have produced a system with basic tools and lessons learned that the reader can easily follow to rebuild their belief system to master the art of decision-making. I hold an executive MBA from London Business School, which I chose to pursue after seventeen years of professional experience in the industry. Also, during my career, I was able to achieve various professional certificates, including Certified Managerial Accountant (CMA), Certified Public Accountant (CPA), and Chartered Financial Analyst (CFA).

I became an audit manager at Ernst & Young in 2007, and then I was selected to lead another department with fourteen team members from seven different countries. One thing these fourteen individuals did was to unanimously vote for me as a true leader, and we worked together to achieve wonders for the company for the next five years before I chose to leave Ernst & Young and start my next adventure.

In 2011, I was well advanced in my career at Ernst & Young and was on my way to becoming a partner when I chose to leave. In the same year, I became a Chief Financial Officer (CFO) at the age of thirty. During my time in the industry, I also served as a group Chief Executive Officer (CEO) for one of the family businesses in the United Arab Emirates (UAE).

During my entire career, I was able to coach, counsel, and mentor many individuals who are today successful in their own careers. There is no greater feeling than receiving a call from an old colleague whom I have helped, sharing news related to his/her achievements, as it gives me a sense of joy and achievement. Even though I had nothing to do with it directly other than giving them advice or guidance, which they really appreciate, I reply by saying, 'Thank you for listening and trusting me to give you advice related to your future, but most importantly, thank you for believing in yourself and taking action'.

What is my true passion, purpose, and cause?

I'm a loving husband and father of three adorable kids. As I write this book, they are growing; in fact, they are growing up fast! But all parents will fully understand the fact that they will always remain kids in our eyes. My larger family includes my parents, two sisters, and two brothers.

My father was forced to leave Palestine at a very young age. However, he persisted in following his dreams and created the right environment to achieve his ambition. If I had to define my father in a statement, I would simply say that he has shown a strong degree of perseverance to achieve all his goals without compromising his principles and identity throughout his entire career and life. Who does not want to control his/her life? Who does not want to sit behind the steering wheel and drive every aspect of his/her life?

I doubt that there is one single human being who will say no. On the contrary, we, as human beings, like (even love) to be in control of our own lives. Being a family-oriented person, the first thing I wanted when I grew up, before achieving anything else, was to get married.

For me, it means the world that I am not alone and that I am with my wife. I wanted to accomplish all my goals in life with her. So, we started from scratch and grew together. We built a lovely family and are still going strong. My sense of purpose is that every one of us has the right to make choices, even in cases that are not personal to us. In our work lives, we also have relationships that are as significant as those from our personal lives.

There are some corporations, for example, that look at employees as machines or robots rather than as human beings. Respect for another human is the element that tends to get lost in the rat race of deadlines and profit margins.

People come with different backgrounds, experiences, cultures, values, ethics, religions, etc., all of which must play a vital role in any relationship a corporation has with its employees.

Setting corporate culture, developing a company's vision and mission statements, policies, and procedures, etc., the values of questioning the status quo, not taking things for granted, giving more, and receiving less—all of this is decided by the executive-level teams.

The simple fact is that we all have value, rights, unique thoughts, and skill sets. Companies must respect that and create an environment that allows their employees to share their uniqueness and value.

If we have the habit of compromising, it means that we don't live up to our expectations. Since I became mature enough to understand things, I have always had and still have a repeating question in my mind, which is simply the word, 'Why?'

The word 'Why?' kept me on the move all my life and did not let me settle for what is less than my worth or what could compromise my values and principles. I'm a big believer in my value and the fact that I deserve to get the same value in return—not more, as that would be greedy, but definitely not less.

During my last year in Oman, I believed I was on the right path to reach the peak of my career and had the opportunity to even grow further, which was supposed to make me happy.

However, I still wasn't fulfilled. There was a feeling of dissatisfaction. Maybe I wanted to understand more about life, to have more experiences, to build new networks and relationships, to go to a bigger market, to learn more about various cultures and corporations, etc.

I simply wanted to find the answer to my question, 'Why?' Now, I was not asking myself why we came to this earth, as I knew that answer and had no doubt in that regard. My 'Why?' was more toward how we are supposed to live our lives. Why are people not satisfied regardless of their stage in life, regardless of their accomplishments?

Why are more people complaining? Why are corporations saying something and doing something else? Why do corporations invest millions in developing corporate values, mission, and vision statements and still fail to build the right culture for their employees? Why do people hate each other?

Answering my 'Why?' made me move to another city. I moved from Muscat to Dubai, a city that, in my opinion, is vibrant and considered to be the most diversified city in the world. Thus, that was definitely a move that would allow me to grow as a person and as a professional at the same time.

This would be a move that would shake me out of my comfort zone and challenge my resourcefulness to the extreme. In my first five years in Dubai, I changed companies four times. These companies were diverse in terms of their legal status, shareholding structure, and nationality. They ranged from publicly listed companies to family businesses from different nations like Afghanistan, UAE, and India.

They all had one thing in common, though. All of them, regardless of their company's maturity, failed to answer my 'Why?' in terms of establishing the right corporate culture where people are first and numbers come second. No wonder that despite their success at certain times, the founders and the shareholders were always under stress to continue restructuring the companies, an exercise that never ended, and an area that I became an expert in.

We all have to make choices every single day that bring us a sense of purpose. For example, when we wake up and are faced with the choice to either go to work or stay home, we unconsciously choose to go to work mainly to satisfy our financial and family commitments. However, there is more to life than just work; it is also about building connections.

To prove a point, let me ask you a question. If someone took your financial commitment away from you, would you still go to work? Will you still go to the same job you have?

The world focuses on staying ahead of the competition, and workers have become nothing more than pawns in the cycle of getting the work done. One day, I heard the term 'corporate slaves'. As much as I hated it, it, unfortunately, felt true. So, another question arises: 'Why is that?'

Choices are always available to us. Nonetheless, how to make them and on what basis is the challenging part, and this is where we fail the most.

I have chosen to write this book to document what I have learned during my career, from my experiences, and from the diverse people I have dealt with at different hierarchies and in different situations, so that the reader can learn and believe that we all have a choice to make (it is our right, without doubt); and that everything matters in our lives.

By sharing my experiences and lessons, I hope to provide you with the future version of you. I hope you use this book as a guide to build your belief system and master the art of decision-making.

The power of choice can't be measured in numbers. However, the power comes from when it has an impact on our lives in a way that signifies its importance.

I was a big failure during my school years, especially in the eyes of my hero, my father. However, following my graduation, something completely changed. It was a 180-degree change. I graduated in marketing as my major in the summer of 2001 with a GPA of 70, and I was lucky enough to join a few interns to work for Nestle on some promotional projects. It happened immediately, the day after completing my last day in college. This opportunity was a daily job where we met every morning at the company headquarters and planned the day's routine. Then, every one of us went in this direction; we had to repeat the same every day for six months.

I mentioned the word 'lucky' earlier because the chances for a graduate like me from a small city far from the capital to get a job was very low. So, I had to capitalize on this opportunity and get the maximum benefit out of it, and this is exactly what I did.

Meanwhile, I kept myself occupied, earned money, and learned something about life. Later in my career, I realized the benefit of such an experience.

As Tony Robbins says, 'Things in life happen for us and not to us'. On the morning of February 12 2002, I was going back to my parents' home after taking the first part of the CMA exam. This was a three-hour online exam, and you get your results immediately after completing it. So, I was on my way back, riding a bus, thinking how I was going to deliver the message of my failure to my parents, especially my father. I didn't want to be a failure in his eyes anymore.

Remember, I was in a full transition in my life. I wanted to change as a person and I was hoping to capitalize on this transitional opportunity to succeed. In addition, my family's financial situation was bad, and my father had to borrow money for me to register for the course and the exam. I had tried my best to study for the exam, but unfortunately, I failed.

I obtained a score of 490, and the passing score was 500. So I was literally so close, but the fact that I didn't pass remained.

I had a choice to make—whether to lie to my father or tell him the truth.

Now, as bad as it might sound, I chose to lie to him. At the back of my mind, I wanted to protect my progress, and all the hard work that I had put toward my exam had to mean something after all. Because in my imagination, telling him I hadn't passed would have caused him to say, 'You will never change despite how many times I supported you'.

By the way, knowing my father, he would never have said that. He kept believing in me for some reason and supported me till the day he passed in 2014. God bless his soul.

Fast forward eight months, I passed all four exams of the CMA and received my qualification. Having this qualification was the main reason I got hired by Ernst & Young in the same month, and that was how I started my career.

I believe that once we make choices, certain things follow, and it's irrelevant whether we call them 'luck' or 'meant to be'. What matters is that we make a choice and end up living the consequences of making them. I remember meeting my future wife and deciding to get married, and things just followed.

Was I ready for a successful marriage at the age of twenty-four, or did I have a perfect plan to avoid the chance of a bad marriage? Of course—but in case you're wondering, I'm still happily married to the same woman I chose, eighteen years and counting.

Just to backtrack a little: it's important to share the decisions that taught me to be who I am today. There was a time I chose to complete two days of work in one day and spend the other day searching academies that taught professional certificates in accounting.

I vividly recall this as if it was yesterday. In that one day, I met this teacher in one of the research academies, and she literally oversold me the same CMA certificate that I later passed.

Maybe she just wanted to sell it to me, but the impact she had on me, without knowing it, was big. I actually left the meeting believing how much my life was going to change if I did get this certificate. Was she exaggerating the reality? Maybe.

At the time, I didn't fully understand the real impact, but now, as I look back on my career and connect the dots, I can simply say, 'Of course not'. And I am grateful that I took that decision, even if I didn't have the complete picture and understanding at the time.

CHOICES LEAD TO HABITS

When I chose to quit smoking, when I chose to leave a partnership career in Ernst & Young, and when I chose to stand by my principles in various critical situations that involved me either risking my job or even quitting, I was actually choosing moments that would shape me; the choices I made were eventually good for my career and life. When I chose to move to Dubai to start all over again after I had built a very successful career in Muscat, there were unknowns that I had to face. When I chose to live my life, when I chose to prioritize my family, when I chose to run my first half-marathon in 2016, when I chose to pursue and finish my CFA against all odds, those experiences created a new mindset in me. When I chose to enroll in LBS to pursue my executive MBA and gained the confidence to start training for triathlon races (specifically Ironman), these choices were moments of truth that gave me a better understanding of my capabilities.

I believe in this: 'Nothing is a greater sacrifice in life more than your freedom'. It is, in fact, my motto.

Having a choice means having control. Having control means having a meaningful life for yourself. What is more important than yourself? If you feel that there are no consequences if you do not take any action, then you are under the delusion that you are taking an easy path through life.

Living your life by default will only cause you pain—if not now, then in the future.

My book is relevant to all decision-makers and will help many, specifically corporate employees struggling with self-awareness, to create change and make choices. Through a system of actionable tools and lessons learned, I provide guidelines to help you unlock the art and the science of decision-making so that you, too, can live a happy, fulfilled, and empowered life.

I believe it's achievable, and you must believe that you too can make choices that will lead you to a better, more fulfilled life.

When we acknowledge that we have a choice and act accordingly, the standards for the quality of our lives rise. As a result, the paradox of choicelessness starts to narrow. This is exactly what we are going to cover in the next chapter. Let's go!

CHAPTER 2

PARADOX OF CHOICELESSNESS

You can't refuse to make a choice

SILENCE IS A STATEMENT; AN INACTION IS AN ACTION BY ITSELF. REFUSING TO MAKE A CHOICE IS A CHOICE.

In this chapter, you will get a taste of what we have ahead in this book. I will share with you experiences I went through in my professional career and personal life that highlight the power of making choices. Making choices has had, and still has, power in my life and that of others. I have produced a system with basic tools and lessons learned from my experiences, so that you can easily follow and rebuild your own belief system to master the art of making decisions. We are constantly making decisions, even if those decisions aren't visible right away; we will realize that they are later. Our choices, whether actively made or not, impact our results.

When I studied for my CFA, I learned that there were always two main strategies any investor can adopt. They can either be active or passive in managing their investments, holding the market variables constant in both cases. The success or failure of either strategy is not the topic of this chapter. What matters is the choice that the investor makes.

If the investor chooses the active strategy, what it means is that they are in the driver's seat and in control of the outcome. If the investor alternatively chooses the passive strategy, their success or failure is solely dependent on the market movement itself. There is no argument that the investor is making a choice in both cases. However, the result of the latter is solely dependent on the market. Being a passive investor or an active one depends on confidence, expertise, and the timing of making the trading decision.

Even though the results obtainable will be impacted by the market, those market factors become secondary. Now think for a moment—even being a passive investor who does nothing is a choice, a choice that investors sometimes make. Learning this made me realize that we follow the same pattern when we make choices in our professional careers and personal lives. Which strategy is better for you? Which strategy brings you greater peace, success, low stress levels, etc.? Which strategy gives you more control over the results?

On February 23 2012, I was called for a meeting with my CEO. At that time, I had newly joined the company as a CFO and was nine months into the job. I had moved into this job after completing my first ten years of professional career in Ernst & Young, so it was my first job as a CFO.

Moving to the industry as a CFO at thirty years of age was a big challenge and a great achievement that I will never take lightly. In that meeting, however, I was called by the CEO to defend a decision, a choice I made on a particular transaction—a transaction I had decided not to approve.

Of course, the CEO didn't accept my decision, so when he called for the meeting, his objective was not to understand why I had made such a decision, but to try to force me into changing it. He didn't even hesitate to invite the company's senior advisor, a retired general in the army who'd co-founded the company, to threaten me and send messages like, 'You are not a team player. Who do you think you are?', 'We run the company, and what we want, we do'. As I remember, the meeting lasted four hours—yes four hours! Mentally, that was the most exhausting experience I ever had to go through in my entire career.

Honestly, when I joined the meeting, it never occurred to me that this was going to happen. In my mind, I thought that it was going to be one of those meetings between a CEO and his CFO; to address business as usual. However, once the first thirty minutes passed, I realized it was bigger than just the decision and the choice I'd made.

From the CEO's perspective, I would be considered a team player only if I had chosen his way and no other way. In the last two hours of the meeting, my mind was flooded with thoughts, 'If I am the CFO and gave the recommendation on this transaction, what did I do wrong? Why's he taking it so personally?

Why this reaction, knowing that my recommendation is only advice and the ultimate decision lies with him?'.

During the meeting, I had no other choice but to listen. Every time I wanted to ask him a question or try to defend my decision, he took it personally, and the conversation got heated.

It reached a point that he pulled himself toward the wall, still sitting in his chair, both hands on his head, and started hitting his head on the wall. It was a shocking reaction.

At that exact point, I realized this was bigger than just a simple debate or an argument between a CFO and a CEO. Basically, he didn't have any tolerance to be told anything otherwise, nor listen to any recommendation that might, in his opinion, delay whatever plans he had. To be honest, his plans were not the company's plans for a reason. That point is beyond the chapter topic, but you get the message.

How did I manage such a meeting? Remember, I was thirty years old, and this was my first experience as a CFO. For me, this meeting could have gone either way. One way was that I ended up having self-doubt; the other way was to end up knowing my true me, my true value.

What made me stronger, I believe, was that I knew my value, my principles, and I remained focused on what was ethically right. I was upset, let us be honest, and it felt easier to accept the CEO's threats and to go along with him and become a team player, to do things his way. But my integrity was in question, and no matter what the consequences were going to be after the meeting, I was mentally ready to accept it and move on.

HOW IT SHAPED ME FOR THE FUTURE AND HOW I MOVED ON

One—I believed that I had to invest more in myself. At the time that I left Ernst & Young at the executive level, I knew I had the skillsets required to do my job. However, I was missing the mindset and the soft skills required to excel in what I did.

Two—I knew I had to protect my integrity no matter what. This is a most intangible benefit, and it is the cost any of us will earn or pay for knowing or not knowing our value.

Three—I learned to lead by example and be a role model who is true to himself.

Four—I learned to keep and improve a sane work ethic mindset.

Five—I learned to manage my thoughts, especially in a negative environment.

Six—I realized that you shouldn't measure people at face value. Intentions are hidden underneath and will always come to the surface with continuous interactions and meetings such as this one.

We all build new capabilities throughout our journey; some inspire us, and by some, we learn to become the better version of ourselves. Basically, it's a one-way process only. There's a 'win way' and nothing else. Do you agree?

There is no denying that we need to continuously work on our skills in order for us to excel in our workplace. However, to master the art of decision-making, the same amount of work, if not more, needs to be done on our mindset. I'm a huge sports fan and an athlete. I diligently study the mindset of pro athletes in different sports, more specifically, tennis, triathlons, and NBA basketball. My passion is always to be the best version of myself and the best role model for my kids, so why not learn from the best athletes in the universe?

At this point, I would like to refer to a presentation by Janne Mortensen at TEDx Talks, Denmark. She explained why a result-oriented approach for an elite athlete is a wrong approach and doesn't guarantee winning if followed. Why is that? A result-oriented approach, she explains, underpins the belief that you have to achieve something for you to be someone. Focusing too much on results is totally counterproductive and puts immense pressure on athletes. She explained that her secret to helping the young talent become the best athlete in his or her sport is by teaching them that you must become *someone* before you become *something.*

According to Mortensen, more often than not, when we refer to becoming someone, we really mean having a status (something). For example, if you want to become number one in a sport, achieving the number one status becomes far more important than what you become during the journey. When you are clear about who you want to be, everything else becomes easier.

When you harness your ability to make decisions, making choices under pressure and in the moment becomes second nature. The focus would always be on who you are, what experiences you have gained, what you have been working on, how you felt, your thoughts, and your plans, rather than centering all your self-expectations on what you have achieved or what you want to achieve.

People often confuse status and value. They believe that they must become something to be someone, and that's not true. You are already a valuable someone. If you can't be fulfilled with nothing, you will never be fulfilled with anything.

Status is what the world gives you, but value is what you are born with. And you nurture your value with all the experiences, lessons, relationships, and so much more you developed during your lifetime. What you have as a person has nothing to do with who you are.

INNER STRENGTH

Mental training is necessary to identify who we really are and who we want to be. The process starts with listing your values and being clear on what each value means to you. Ultimately, when you focus on your value and not results, it guarantees you becoming the best version of yourself. As you go through this book, keep asking yourself this question: 'Is it worth it to compromise what feels right for me to satisfy others?'.

ROADMAP

The roadmap of the book will be simple. We have seven lessons.

Lesson one: Know your value, and it's not negotiable.

Lesson two: How to live up to your own expectations.

Lesson three: Know how to prioritize wisely.

Lesson four: Your mindset is your success. Learn how to strengthen it.

Lesson five: Know that not taking action is an action by itself.

Lesson six: How to communicate with your audience.

Lesson seven: How to navigate obstacles and keep progressing.

I would like to conclude with the fact that life is all about choices, even if we don't feel so at times. From the moment we wake up in the morning, we start with making a choice whether to make our bed, brush our teeth, say good morning to our significant other, and so on. If life is basically all about making choices, why not master making them?

I'm about to take you on a journey to teach you the skillset and required mindset to master the art of decision-making. Let's go!

CHAPTER 3

LESSON #1:
KNOW YOUR VALUE

Know your value + Be authentic = Your success

You have a value to share with others. Imagine that you are talking to your son. What would be the best advice you could give him when he is about to enter into an interview, or a meeting, or start something meaningful in his life?

In my experience, most of us, if not all, will say these two words: 'Be yourself'. Because we know that the best result any person can get from any interaction is by being themselves.

This makes me wonder. Despite knowing that 'being yourself' will get you the best results, we don't even consciously put in the effort required to know who we really are and what our true value is.

By the end of this chapter, you'll be able to establish the belief that you have a value, and that value drives all your choices. We will conclude that value is not constant, and rises over time depending on how we treat it and take care of it. Therefore, you must know it, acknowledge it, appreciate it, protect it, and invest in it.

In this chapter, you will learn the foundational equation of success. Knowing your value leads to your authenticity, which leads to your success.

WHAT IS VALUE?

What are the main four drivers of our value? As you can see below, they are:

1. Our own values, principles, and boundaries
2. Our experiences
3. Our talent
4. Our skills

Our values are important to us, as they are a reflection of our ultimate behavior. Our values encompass our beliefs, our principles, the way we were raised, what we see as right and wrong, what is acceptable and forbidden to us, etc. By these values, we live with dignity, and we develop our own personal beliefs and convictions.

In an organizational context, the values of a company are the product of a detailed analysis conducted by management after considering the company's mission and vision statements. This has to be communicated to every employee, and there is a need to ensure that every employee understands and adapts these values in order for the company to achieve its strategic objectives.

For easy reference, I have inserted below a Venn diagram that shows these main drivers, with our value being simply the ultimate interaction between these four drivers.

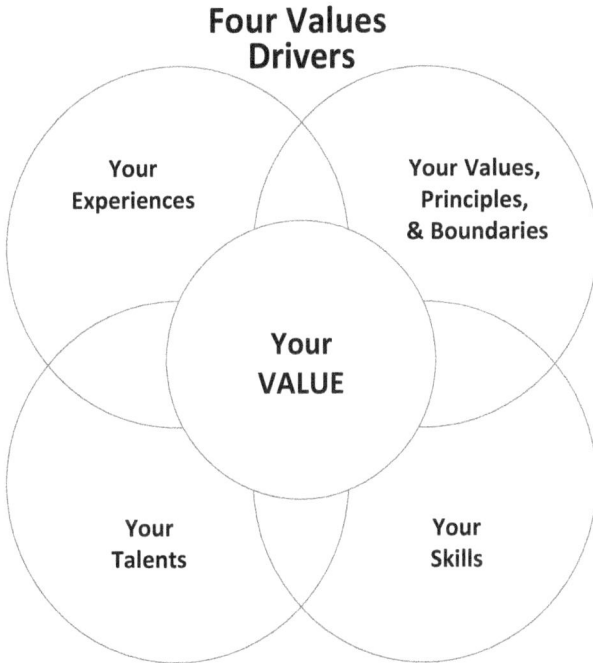

Four Values Drivers

Your Experiences

Your Values, Principles, & Boundaries

Your VALUE

Your Talents

Your Skills

Our experiences come from daily interactions with people around us, whether family members or strangers, from what we expose ourselves to in our professional and personal lives, including traveling to different cities and countries, etc.

These experiences are the building blocks for us to become who we are. They can be likened to the sharpener that shapes our knowledge and level of maturity when dealing with others.

Our talent is associated with us from the day we are born; every single person is gifted with a particular talent. Finding that talent is not easy, and one of the advantages of knowing your value is that it will help you discover it. Talent is like any other muscle in our body; it requires continuous training to develop, master, and maintain.

Our skills come from continuous practice and execution. As we all know, skills are either technical or soft. Technical skills are more tangible than soft skills, meaning that they can be evaluated easily, and we can put up a plan to develop them. On the other hand, soft skills are more intangible; they require extra effort to understand and an immense amount of practice and execution to master.

There is one important topic I would like to highlight here, which I drew from the financial literature, and that is 'the effect of compounding'. Let's assume that you are an asset class that you decided to invest in. Before you make the investment, you have a value of X, resulting from your values, past experiences, principles, etc., and now you decided to invest more into yourself by getting into a new experience in life or through new learning. We will all agree that your value will increase after this new experience or learning. This can be equated to X+1 in value terms. However, what is interesting about the effect of compounding is that this new value gets magnified even more. With continuous improvements, extra skills, and new education, your value magnifies over time and has a greater impact on the person you can become. In other words, 1 plus 1 does not equal 2!

A compounding effect happens when you decide to reinvest income already generated in the same asset class to provide greater potential for profits. This is also known as 'Interest on interest'.

There are two problems associated with us not knowing our value, and these are acceptance and confidence. To know your value, you need to strengthen your self-acceptance and self-confidence. This book is your guide to show you how.

THE TOUGH CHOICES

Have you ever been in the middle of an interview or a situation where you felt, 'Oh, I don't want to be here, or I shouldn't be here?' All the negative thoughts start to come to your mind, and you feel that you have ruined the interview despite being prepared.

Let me talk about an instance that took place in August 2016. I was the group CFO for a company, and I was called for a meeting with my group CEO concerning an email I had sent that morning (a choice I made) on a particular transaction related to the company's strategy.

To give you a little background, the CEO and I had met a few months earlier, along with the company's CIO (Chief Investment Officer), to work on the company's long-term strategy, and I had presented an idea for a merger transaction that was highly welcomed by the CEO and the team.

Our group CEO was an emotional person and a great leader. His emotions sometimes influenced his decisions, in the short term at least. So, during our regular meetings update, I had to highlight the risks involved in the strategy along with the benefits.

He hated the risks, of course, but I had to do my job to remind him about them as we progressed. Even then, I had the feeling that I was not delivering the full picture to him verbally, as he was always trying to avoid the risks and moving forward as if these possibilities didn't exist; he simply didn't want to let go of the idea.

My email that morning, after a huge amount of diligence, of course, basically addressed more concerns and risks associated with that idea. And I recommended a different way of execution. The email was simply another method of communication. I provided my analysis of the idea and sent it to both the Group Chief Executive Officer and CIO because I thought if they just read it without any emotions or verbal noises, it might resonate and let them see it through my lens.

In the time leading to the email, I had dug deep into the idea, as any decision we make in life has its own advantages and disadvantages. But I believed in what I did and never doubted my confidence level.

However, when the GCEO read the email, he saw it from a different perspective, thought I was completely out of my mind, and was trying to change my position on the strategy. He got frustrated, which I realized as soon as I entered his office.

The agenda of the meeting was simply to get me fired or ruin my reputation. I went through another tough meeting, which I will explain below, but guess what?

A few months later, in December of that year, I scored the highest in my performance appraisal from the same GCEO, and I was considered the top performer in the company. From that year onward, we built the most successful relationship that any CFO and CEO could ever imagine.

During my entire career, I always believed that I should speak my views and give recommendations as I see fit, no matter what the circumstances are. Of course, being methodical myself, I do my thorough due diligence before I give any recommendation.

How did I manage such a meeting, and more importantly, how was I able to change the GCEO's mind in a few months?

One—By taking deep breaths and staying calm during that meeting.

Two—I stayed confident and remained focused on my message. As you can relate, the email I sent was taken out of context, which was completely opposite to the plan. Nonetheless, I kept going back to the main topic of the transaction.

Three—I tried to focus on the solution and the fact that it was my idea in the first place. Simply addressing its risks was not supposed to change the idea or the decision; it was only to highlight them, as it might require us to change the execution plan.

Four—I remained positive along the way and ignored the negative messages from my colleague. This was a very hard step. However, with confidence and acceptance and my level of preparation, I was able to remain positive.

Five—I didn't leave the meeting without agreeing on short-term actions that I was supposed to take. I also agreed to be held responsible in case I failed. I did my homework, remember.

HOW IT SHAPED ME FOR THE FUTURE

1. I knew I had to keep investing in myself. Because the more I invest, the more I become skilled in many aspects. My confidence and value automatically rise, which helps me add value to others.
2. I knew I needed to continue taking risks and making decisions. I learned not to leave things without a decision. Circumstances keep changing, and we can't afford not to make decisions.
3. I learned not to get intimidated by the situation, even if it had implications. For instance, the scenario I presented earlier had implications for my employment, which was that I could have lost my job or worse.

4. All of the above was driven by having confidence and acceptance of the situation, the challenge, and the outcome.

IDENTIFY THE PROBLEM

So long as you are dependent on others to define you, you'll always be at their mercy. You'll become the follower and not the leader. Then, in that case, imagine how your future will be? Are you in control?

I like to call it, 'You're being abused'.

Always remember that when you don't know the value of something, you are bound to abuse it, simply because we are human, and this is what humans do, right?

People will value you to the degree you value yourself. People will respect you to the degree you respect yourself. People will love you to the degree you love yourself.

WHAT DOES ACCEPTANCE MEAN?

It means embracing yourself in all aspects—the strengths and weaknesses that you have, when you are at your best and when you are at your worst. Tony Robbins said, *'When you know yourself, you are empowered, but when you accept yourself, you're invincible'*. Accepting yourself is the foundation for your greatness. Why? Because it influences three things.

1. Acceptance influences the way you give meaning.
2. Acceptance influences the way you think.
3. Acceptance influences the way you respond.

TRUST IN SELF

Confidence, on the other hand, is a feeling of self-assurance regarding your capabilities, meaning that you know that you are enough.

The goal is to get you to believe how great you are regardless of how others see you. Confidence is a true reflection of knowing who you are.

It reduces fear, worry, and self-doubt. If you know that you are well-equipped to face your difficulties, you don't worry about being broken down or not being able to accomplish things. It all starts with the mindset, and the right mindset starts from confidence.

Confidence also translates into knowing yourself and understanding the situation you are about to face. It allows you to be the maestro to control any situation.

Whether in life or at work, we will always have to communicate with others. Don't ever start a communication from an argumentative standpoint. Rather, start by knowing your value, and your perspective. Don't get caught in the 'I am right, you are wrong' narrative. A proper consideration of differing viewpoints is key. To be properly considered, you need to know your value.

Don't just focus on tangibles, the bonus, the salary, or the perks. The intangibles, such as your soft skills, matter too. To be properly considered, people need to be learning from you. It's not one-way traffic. People must learn from you just as you learn from them as well.

You must operate from your authenticity, your passion, and your purpose. *Yours,* not theirs.

Get clarity about your vision. Be clear on where you are and where you want to go. We tend to underestimate the power of having a clear vision. Meanwhile, having a clear vision of what you want gives you the power to be yourself and make choices even when you are faced with obstacles (which is in every case of our lives).

Having a clear vision allows you to make choices spontaneously. You are able to give every obstacle you face a proper meaning and figure out how it relates to you so you can act in a way that will benefit you. Some may call it luck or something else; however, I call it the power of having clear vision.

The time you spend on really understanding your vision is valuable, so take your time. It makes the subsequent steps easier.

Only after you are crystal-clear about your vision should you set your goals, both short and long-term. Nothing in life can be achieved without goals. Goals are like milestones. Once we achieve one, we celebrate it and move to the next one.

From experience, writing your goals down makes them real, and this is exactly what you should do. Write all your goals on a piece of paper and stick it on the wall or any other place. You can also write them on your laptop. It doesn't matter. What matters is that you write them down.

Next, assign deadlines to each goal and schedule them in your calendar. Then, share a plan with your significant other or someone who can hold you accountable. At the end of the day, you need support/encouragement along the way.

Continue moving and achieving your goals one by one, as this gives you the drive and the motivation to keep going.

Creating momentum is crucial for success. Share your plan with the relevant parties. Without supervision, we tend to become easy on ourselves. Remember, the foundational formula for success is to know your value and be authentic.

Before you jump to the next chapter, take a pen and paper and ask yourself these questions.

1. Am I really clear about my vision?
2. Am I really clear about my goals?
3. Do I hold myself accountable?

4. Do I know my value and act on it?
5. What are my values? (Write these in a separate list.)

Write down your principles. Write down your boundaries.

Start with 'I will never …'

So often in life, there is a mismatch between our expectations and the level we rise to. This creates some discord within us and affects how we relate with others. Let's talk about it in the next chapter.

CHAPTER 4

LESSON #2:
HOW TO LIVE UP TO
YOUR EXPECTATIONS

Your promises to yourself are far more important than any other promise you make!

PERSONAL AND PROFESSIONAL SATISFACTION ONLY COMES FROM MEASURING OUTCOMES, WHICH IS DEPENDENT ON SETTING EXPECTATIONS.

When was the last time you made yourself a promise but didn't follow through? I think all of us have done that.

Promises can be as simple as telling yourself, 'I will follow a diet to take care of my health'. Or it can be as complex as a long-term plan to compete in the Iron Man World Championship. Regardless of the type of promises you make to yourself, you need to do the required work.

The feeling that completing a promise leaves behind is bad and eventually reduces our self-esteem. I remember when I chose to pursue my CFA in 2008. I was able to pass Part 1 and 2 of the CFA in six months, in December 2008 and June 2009, respectively. However, I failed to pass CFA Part 3 until June 2016 for so many reasons. Some of these were my fault, and some years, I didn't even register for the exam. But, I always felt I was failing myself because I was not trying enough to study and do the required work to finish up and gain that CFA status. There are three exams that you must complete, and I'd done two out of three. I should have been proud, but because I promised myself to become a CFA holder, it didn't feel right until I accomplished it.

The moral of the story is that you have to keep pushing yourself to stay firm in your own values. There are certain things outside of our control that can push us backward. But from this experience, if you keep your promises to yourself, you end up achieving them even if it takes more time than expected. Achieving this objective or promise will make you that much prouder. The benefit that you gain in the way of confidence in yourself is double or even triple the impact of not keeping the promise and failing to live up to your expectations.

In this chapter, we will discuss how to set your expectations, create a plan, and set milestones, step by step, to enable you to achieve and live up to those expectations. By the end of this chapter, you will know why setting expectations is paramount. You will be able to assess whether you are living up to your expectations, know why you should be doing so, and understand how that is relevant to mastering choice-making, which is what we are trying to establish in this book.

EXPECTATIONS

Now, have you ever treated yourself as someone under your supervision? Would you set expectations for yourself in that case or not? Most probably, the answer would be 'Yes', because it's impossible to measure any performance without clear expectations being set.

WHY WE HAVE TO SET EXPECTATIONS

When we talk about setting expectations, the first thing we need to do is to define and understand what expectation means. An expectation can be defined as what you want from yourself on a particular day or a particular job or a particular relationship. It can be a milestone goal that you want to achieve. Expectations are also driven by what others expect from you when we define it in a relationship or in a job. Expectations could even be things you promise yourself to achieve; thus, this comes from within you, and you set expectations for yourself based on your purpose.

If your expectations are not clear, there is a lot of emotional energy that is wasted through anxiety and the stress of uncertainty. As human beings, we love certainty. We love knowing, and we are motivated to work toward something if we know what that something is. Uncertainty fills us with fear. When we feel fear, we consequently feel insecure. Even if we have promises that we made to ourselves along the way, uncertainty, sometimes if not most of the time, kills the journey by making us stop because we disbelieve our abilities. So, as human beings, we love having certainty. Certainty is key; it is essential when we talk about setting expectations. Having clarity means you one hundred percent know what you want.

And as explained in previous chapters and throughout this book, clarity comes from knowing your purpose. It comes from having a vision and setting goals for yourself. This clarity is what you need when you set expectations.

More specifically, you need to be clear on the 'What' and the 'Why?'.

I would like to ask a question here. When we enter into relationships, do you think we enter such relationships without any expectations from each other? Even if we don't write them on a piece of paper, expectations exist, and we judge ourselves according to them. We simply expect certain things from the other party, and vice versa. For instance, in parental relationships, we have certain expectations of our kids when they go to school, even when we don't mention or discuss these expectations. Now, whether we write them down on a piece of paper or hang them on the refrigerator does not change the fact that we actually set expectations. Therefore, it is essential to master the art of setting expectations, especially our own.

RESPONSIBILITY AND ACCOUNTABILITY

One critical aspect here, and it's a fact, is that you can't achieve success in setting expectations without having both responsibility and accountability. Whether you assign someone else to hold you accountable is not the point here. The point is that your accountability must come from your inside. This level of commitment and dedication in you is essential not only to ensure that you achieve your goals or expectations, but also for the attitude of positivity that it creates. It becomes more about the positive emotions that you create for yourself during the journey. You feel proud of yourself, and that, by itself, is a positive emotion that gives you courage, increases your confidence, lifts your self-esteem, and keeps you moving forward from one milestone to another milestone. And this is how you stay focused and rising. We must learn to reward ourselves for every promise, goal, or expectation that we achieve or reach, no matter how little they are.

Also, as human beings, rewarding ourselves for promises we made true makes us feel happy. When you pat your shoulder after achieving a promise, it empowers you to realize and acknowledge that what you have achieved is great, and that you are on the track to success. Saluting ourselves is important to go to the next level.

Life is a journey; it's not only one milestone before you stop. As human beings, we must keep moving and pushing. We have several milestones during our journey, and it is by conquering them that we keep rising and growing in our careers and personal lives.

CAREER CONNECTION

In the context of corporates, if leaders want to maximize employees' productivity, get projects completed on time and accurately, and help the business thrive, they must ensure that every team member understands exactly what is expected of them. However, setting clear expectations is sometimes easier said than done, and there are 'right' ways and 'wrong' ways to do so. Whether they are unintentionally unclear, expect too much, or come across as micromanaging, a lot can go wrong when a leader tries to clarify for employees what is expected of them.

I read an article written by members of Forbes Coaches Council, where they discussed twelve 'right' ways to set expectations with employees. I would like to highlight the majority of them below.

1. Provide clarity, context, and alignment. Setting expectations is critical in leadership, and research shows that many executives are overlooking this key element. When setting expectations with employees, giving context is key. Knowing the why, and how they play an integral role in the organization's strategic objectives allows for greater commitment to the work and to the team.

2. Speak in plain words that create a positive impact. Communicating in simple, plain words is key. Also, listening to employees during the expectation-setting sessions is important, as it allows for better alignment between their perception and what is meant to be delivered.

3. Ask rather than instruct. Executives who adopt a coaching approach and ask questions, rather than giving instructions on what needs to be done, will get better commitment from their employees.

4. Seek continuous feedback. High performance can be achieved with constant communication and feedback from employees.

5. Be open about what expectations are and why. The right way to set expectations with employees is to help them understand their role and scope of work. Also, offer the flexibility for employees to explore their own skills within their tasks and ensure that expectations are attainable. The best way to set expectations for employees is to make the goals reachable and in alignment with the mission and vision of the company. Expectations must be beneficial for the success of the organization.

6. Partner with the employees when setting expectations. Make it a partnership, which will ensure a sense of commitment within the team and a motivation to do their jobs. Find out if they are clear on the expectations of their roles. What are their ideas for achieving their expectations? How would they measure their performance? This process of enquiry helps to build their confidence and encourages them to set the bar higher to achieve even more.

7. Ask about employees' personal goals. What do they want to achieve? How far are they looking to go in their careers? Do they want to upskill themselves? All these questions ensure that the employee's mindset is on a positive trajectory.

8. Communicate the vision clearly and simply. Communicate the organization's vision and team goals clearly. Then, go one step further to break it down, aligning the goals to their role. Let them understand how their roles relate to the organization's vision and mission.

9. Explain and prioritize KPIs (Key Performance Indicators) from the start. The right way to set expectations with employees is to explain the KPI and prioritize them from the beginning.

10. Set the rapport and tone with a positive frame of mind. As an executive, it is your responsibility to establish a rapport with your employees.

11. Trust your employees to be keen to meet expectations. Combine the expectations with a genuine belief that your team can and will achieve what is expected of them.

EXPECTATIONS ARE A PART OF LIFE

As individual parents, we all remember how we unconsciously set expectations for our kids when they started going to school, whether we communicated these with them or not. Such expectations would be that they attend all classes, concentrate well, study hard, and achieve great marks. But how many times did we actually sit with our kids to lay down our expectations?

Setting clear expectations can be incredibly beneficial in helping us take control of our lives. When we set expectations, we create a roadmap for our actions and decisions, which leads to the following advantages:

1. **Clarity:** Expectations provide a clear vision of what we want to achieve, helping us prioritize our goals and focus on what truly matters.
2. **Motivation:** Defined expectations can serve as a source of motivation, as they give us a target to strive for and a sense of purpose.
3. **Direction:** Expectations act as a compass, guiding us through challenges and uncertainties by providing a sense of direction and purpose.
4. **Decision-making:** Having clear expectations makes decision-making more straightforward, as we can evaluate options based on whether they align with our goals or not.
5. **Personal growth:** Setting expectations challenges us to grow and improve as we aim to meet or exceed the standards we've set for ourselves.
6. **Accountability:** Expectations make us more accountable for our actions and results, encouraging us to take responsibility for our choices.
7. **Reduced stress:** Knowing what we expect from ourselves and others can reduce stress because it eliminates ambiguity and unpredictability.

Examples of setting expectations to control our lives:

1. **Career:** Define your career expectations, such as achieving a specific position, acquiring certain skills, or aiming for a salary level. These expectations can guide your career choices and professional development.
2. **Relationships:** Set expectations, such as open communication, mutual respect, and shared responsibilities in your relationships. This helps foster healthier and more fulfilling connections with others.
3. **Health and fitness:** Establish expectations, such as exercising regularly, eating a balanced diet, and getting enough sleep for your health and fitness goals. These expectations can lead to a healthier lifestyle.
4. **Personal projects:** When starting a personal project, set clear expectations for what you want to achieve, the steps to take, and a timeline for completion.
5. **Financial management:** Set expectations for your financial goals, such as saving a certain amount each month, avoiding unnecessary expenses, and planning for long-term financial stability.
6. **Learning and education:** Establish expectations for your learning journey, such as taking up new courses, reading a specific number of books, or improving knowledge in a particular field.
7. **Time management:** Set expectations for managing your time, prioritizing tasks, avoiding procrastination, and allocating time for leisure and self-care.

By setting expectations in these and other areas of life, you gain greater control over your actions and choices, leading to a more fulfilling and purpose-driven life. Therefore, it goes without saying that mastering the setting of expectations is essential to success in all areas of our lives.

As I recall, I was not the perfect kid in school. To be completely honest, I was a disaster, especially in the eyes of my father and others in the family. For example, when I was in Grade Twelve studying to graduate high school and get into university, I was far behind in my studies. I knew that if I put in the effort required to achieve a grade above a certain threshold (but, of course, not the high score everyone was anticipating), I could apply to the university and get accepted into the Business Administration college, and that's exactly what I did. So, I set an expectation for myself and worked toward it because it was very clear in my mind. Unfortunately, it was not a type of achievement that made my father or family proud, but nonetheless, I made him proud in the later stages of my career.

I studied accounting in college as my major for the first two years. And once the school announced the opening for a new major, marketing, I simply moved. To be honest, it was for silly reasons; nonetheless, I wanted something new, as accounting books seemed rigid, and I wanted something that had life in it. As unplanned as this may sound, there was a hidden promise I made to myself that year, and it was that I wanted to finish in two years and be the first to graduate from the college with a marketing degree. And guess what? This is exactly what happened.

The lesson learned from these two examples that I gave is that we set expectations even if we don't speak about them. And because we know ourselves, it's very clear to us, even if it is not so to others, even our closest family members. Our expectations are why we do things the way we do them, why we participate in certain events and avoid others. It is just because they relate to us, our personalities, our purpose, and the way we define our lives.

When it comes to setting expectations, a lot of them come unspoken. By sharing my experiences, I want to raise awareness and make it more process-oriented. Most of the time, obstacles in life, unfortunately, hold us back, and we move our focus from the journey we are on. Setting expectations in a process-oriented manner helps us to keep that focus along the way.

For this to work, follow these steps to master setting your expectations right:

1. **Self-reflection:** Take some time to reflect on your values, priorities, and long-term goals. Understand what truly matters to you and what you want to achieve in various aspects of your life.
2. **Be realistic:** Set expectations that are achievable and realistic. Avoid setting goals that are too ambitious or

beyond your current capabilities, as they might lead to frustration and disappointment.

3. **Specificity:** Be clear and specific about what you expect from yourself and others. Vague expectations can lead to misunderstandings and unmet goals.

4. **Write them down:** Put your expectations in writing. Whether it's in a journal, a planner, or digital notes, having your expectations documented makes them more tangible and helps you track progress.

5. **Communicate:** If your expectations involve other people, communicate them openly and honestly. Clearly explain what you expect and be open to feedback and negotiation.

6. **Break them down:** Divide your expectations into smaller, manageable tasks or milestones. This makes the process less overwhelming and allows you to track your progress more effectively.

7. **Set timeframes:** Assign a realistic timeline to each expectation. Having deadlines can help create a sense of urgency and keep you focused on achieving your goals.

8. **Monitor progress:** Regularly review your progress towards meeting your expectations. If you're falling behind, assess what needs to be adjusted and make necessary changes.

9. **Be flexible:** Understand that life is unpredictable, and circumstances may change. Be willing to adapt your expectations when needed while staying true to your core values and long-term goals.

10. **Celebrate achievements:** Acknowledge and celebrate your successes along the way. Recognizing your accomplishments boosts motivation and reinforces positive emotions.

11. **Learn from setbacks:** If you face setbacks or encounter challenges, view them as learning opportunities. Analyze what went wrong and use that knowledge to adjust your approach moving forward.
12. **Practice patience:** Setting expectations takes time, and achieving them may not happen overnight. Be patient with yourself and others as you work towards your goals.

By taking these actions, you'll be well on your way to setting your expectations right and creating a more fulfilling and purposeful life.

Keep repeating the above steps so they become a habit. Then, add, revise, and revisit expectations as you grow and evolve. Life evolves, too, and the only constant in life is change. Work on your adaptation skills. We must be flexible and adapt to the new norm. When the Coronavirus hit us in 2020, nobody knew what it was and no-one knew how to deal with it. But as human beings, we survived it, and we thrived post-COVID-19.

Now that we have mastered the skill of setting our expectations, the next step will be to prioritize them and maximize our resources and potential. Let's talk about it in the next chapter.

CHAPTER 5

LESSON # 3: KNOW HOW TO PRIORITIZE

Your long-term vision is your number one priority!

UNDERSTANDING YOUR PRIORITIES AND ACTING ON THEM MEANS GIVING YOURSELF PERMISSION TO CHART A PATH TOWARD WEALTH AND FREEDOM.

When was the last time you failed yourself? How many times did you feel you were not going anywhere or that nothing was being accomplished? If you take a moment to think about this, what would be your answer? Do you also agree that setting priorities is important to your success? If so, how are you approaching this in your life? Are your priorities the same as your commitments?

First, let us start with what priority means. Priority comes from importance. If you consider a task high priority, this means it's highly important to you. The importance of the activity is a relative measure to any of us. What is important to me may not be important to you, and vice versa. But where does this importance come from? The answer is because it brings us toward achieving our goals.

By the end of this chapter, you will be able to assess the importance of mastering the art of setting priorities and learn how setting priorities is the number one driver that allows us to achieve our goals and, to the best of our knowledge, have control over the outcome.

We all agree that knowing how to prioritize is key. We are going to prove this in this chapter and find out how this is correlated with our success.

First, it provides you the needed focus.

Second, it gives you the ability to control and manage your time more efficiently.

Third, you become more productive.

Fourth, it gives you the momentum of progress.

Fifth, it helps you overcome obstacles in a smart way, not the hard way.

HOW TO PRIORITIZE

Ask yourself this question. What happens if you don't prioritize? How will your life look? Imagine if you are facing multiple decisions to make, and you consider all of them to be equally important. How do you think you will handle them? The answer most probably would be you will end up having a conflict and feeling confusion about all of them. And you end up doing nothing. If all your decisions are equally important, there is a high chance that you will stay still and do nothing. If you're a person who has a bigger will than the rest, you might still do something, but what are the chances of following through with your decision? No priorities means no finish line, and that only adds more stress and anxiety.

To be effective in setting priorities, keep it simple and straightforward by following these steps.

1. Start with listing all your priorities versus all your commitments.
2. Map the priorities you listed with your commitments and understand the overall picture and how they are interlinked.
3. Assign the relative importance to your priorities.
4. Assign the relative urgency to your priorities.
5. You will end up creating a quadrant that has importance and urgency as two quadrants and all your priorities are spotted at different places in the graph.
6. Your focus will start with the most important and urgent priority, and it will reduce as you go down in the graph.

7. Break down your priorities into goals, tasks, and milestones.
8. Schedule the time. Put the deadline for all these goals, tasks, and milestones, whether short, medium, or long term.
9. Keep reevaluating.

And finally, keep the following in mind.

First, be disciplined. You need to make the above a habit. It is by being repetitive that we reach mastery level.

Second, understand the fact that we have only got one priority to complete.

The biggest reason people don't achieve their goals is because they set multiple priorities at once. Karen Martin, in her book, *The Outstanding Organization: Generate Business Results by Eliminating Chaos and Building the Foundation for Everyday Excellence,* says, 'When several things are priority, nothing is priority'.

Third, don't start working on a new goal until you accomplish the previous one.

NOT TIME MANAGEMENT

Now, it's critical to highlight that setting priorities is not the same as time management. Setting priorities is more related to an individual's vision in life. It is about what really drives you, what helps you stay focused on what matters and leave out what doesn't. When we have a vision, we become more productive in the twenty-four hours available to us on a daily basis. Having a vision (the big picture) is like glue for all the milestones we want to reach in life.

This vision gives a sense of meaning to all our priorities. Once some things are more important to us than others, we have clarity when we break down our priorities into goals, small daily tasks, and milestones that we need to do to stay on track. Setting priorities requires shifting perspective, as it will shape your life to one that will give you a sense of fulfillment and accomplishment. It is not about how you do a particular task; it's about choosing the right task for you, one that is aligned with your goal, your priority, the meaning that you give to it, and the importance to your life.

Creating priorities can be a challenging task, but it is essential if you want to unleash your 'inner you' and take control of your life. The first step in creating a priority is identifying what matters most to you. This could be your health, relationships, career, or any other aspect of your life that you value. Once you have identified these priorities, the next step is to create a plan that aligns with them. This means setting goals and creating a schedule, a timetable that allows you to focus on the things that matter the most. The key to mastering the art of creating priorities is discipline. It is important to stick to your plan and stay focused on your goals, even when distractions arise. This requires saying no to the things that don't serve your greater purpose and making time for the things that do. By doing so, you can create a life that is aligned with your values and goals and unleash your 'inner you' in the process.

Another key step in mastering the art of prioritization is to identify your core values. This means taking a deep look at what really matters to you and what drives you. Once you have identified these values, you can begin to prioritize your goals and activities accordingly. Remember, it's not just about what you want to achieve, but also about why you want to achieve it. Finally, it is important to regularly check and evaluate your progress and adjust your priorities as needed. You must be adaptable. Life is constantly changing, so it's important to be flexible and adaptable to stay focused and achieve your objective.

When it comes to setting priorities in my personal life, I have a list that I have created: I am a group CFO who works a minimum of ten hours a day, and I have a beautiful wife and three kids whom I prioritize. I also prioritize writing my first book. I am following my dream to become a life coach and working on developing my coaching business in the near future. Plus, I'm a triathlete who dreams of completing Iron Man races across the world, which means I also have to find time for training. To this end, I need long hours of specialized training. And don't forget that I must sleep.

Having said that, I follow the following steps with no fail.

1. Fill my calendar with all my plans. Once I schedule my plan a week ahead, it becomes a reality, and my brain and body start to think in that direction.
2. I stay disciplined. I don't negotiate with myself concerning the timings that I put in the calendar. It can be very hard at the beginning, but once you keep progressing, it becomes a habit, and this is what we want to reach.
3. Whatever my goal is, I must make it a habit. As we said, habits are operated at the unconscious level of the brain, which means you stop thinking about it too often.

When you begin to consider your list, start with the most important, the urgent priorities. And then stay disciplined and make it a habit.

Of course, there is always the argument that when you stay disciplined and do things in a repetitive manner, it becomes a habit, so your unconscious mind starts doing it without even thinking and feeling that it is an effort. At the same time, there is an argument that you also become better at it. So, whether you become better at it or it becomes a habit, both serve the same purpose. Both help you to stay disciplined. You don't think about these things when you do them. So, it is in your favor that you become better at it because of repetition.

PRIORITY vs. COMMITMENT

Priority and commitment are two distinct concepts, although they can often be interconnected. It is important to understand the difference between them and align priorities with commitments. Don't be driven only by commitments. I reflect on what matters to my life and the things that are important to me, and the things that are aligned with my values, purpose, and passion in life. Commitments are always there. You must prioritize them, but their importance should always come from your priorities.

Priority refers to the order in which tasks, goals, or activities are ranked based on their importance and/or urgency. Commitment is a personal or interpersonal pledge or promise to carry out a specific task, duty, or responsibility. It involves a sense of dedication and obligation.

Priorities can change over time, depending on the circumstances, new information, or shifting goals. They can be adjusted to accommodate changing needs or situations. When you make a commitment, you are expected to follow through and fulfill your promise, even if it requires effort or sacrifices.

Setting priorities involves making choices about what should be done first or what deserves more attention and resources. Commitments hold individuals accountable for their actions, and failure to meet them can have consequences for trust and reputation.

Establishing priorities is a crucial aspect of effective time management. It helps you allocate your time and energy to focus on the most critical tasks or goals. Commitment often involves emotional involvement and a strong sense of dedication to seeing a task or goal through to completion.

Priorities are often organized in a hierarchical manner, where some items are deemed more important than others. Commitments are typically enduring and may extend over an extended period. They often require consistency and perseverance.

GET CLARITY OF GOALS

So now that we have determined the importance of making priorities, we know for a fact that there is no progress without priorities. So, what do we need to do? First, you must replace smart goals with clear goals. Clear goals allow for agile thinking and are more attuned to the way human beings work. In CLEAR goals, **C** stands for Collaborative (goals should encourage collaboration). **L** stands for Limited (goals should be limited in both scope and duration). **E** stands for Emotional (goals should make emotional connections). **A** stands for Appreciable (Large goals should be broken into small goals so they can be accomplished more quickly and easily for long-term gain). **R** stands for Refinable (give yourself permission to refine and modify your goals). These are according to an article in the Daily Digest for Entrepreneurs and Business Leaders.

We started this book questioning and asking ourselves: Why? I want you also to keep this self-query as a repetitive habit. A few more questions I would like to raise here are:

1. What do you get emotional about?
2. Which goals have meaning to you?
3. What priorities will get you there?

These tough questions keep your brain in a livable condition, ready when you face situations that are happening to you, and impact the way that you respond to them. The greater impact, though, is the way that you set your priorities and define each priority, the relative importance of it, and the relative urgency of the priority itself. Keep questioning and ask yourself questions to get accuracy. Find out whether it was the 'Why' or whether it was the 'What'.

TAKE ACTION

Take some time to work through and create your own matrix to achieve your own priorities. Results come from allowing yourself to take action. To show you, I will explain by exploring the differences between our financial commitments and having financial freedom as a priority.

Financial commitment and the priority of being financially free are interconnected but represent different aspects of achieving financial stability and freedom.

Financial commitment refers to the promises or obligations you make to allocate your financial resources, including money, time, or effort, toward specific financial goals or activities. It involves setting clear and tangible financial objectives, like paying off debt, saving for retirement, investing in education, or buying a house.

Making financial commitments often requires creating a budget, setting aside a portion of your income for savings or investments, and consistently following through on your financial plan. It holds you accountable for managing your finances responsibly and avoiding impulsive spending that could hinder your progress. Achieving financial commitments may involve making short-term sacrifices, such as cutting unnecessary expenses or delaying gratification, to achieve long-term financial goals.

The priority of being financially free depends on the importance you assign to achieving financial independence and security in your overall life goals. Prioritizing financial freedom means making conscious choices that align with your desire for financial stability. It involves considering your financial wellbeing as a critical factor in making life decisions.

When financial freedom is a priority, you might opt for simpler living, avoid excessive debt, and invest in experiences or assets that contribute to long-term financial security. Making financial freedom a priority requires envisioning your future financial state and taking gradual steps to achieve it. It may require sacrificing some immediate desires in exchange for long-term financial security and peace of mind.

In summary, financial commitment involves setting and adhering to specific financial goals and actions, whereas prioritizing financial freedom means considering financial security as a fundamental aspect of your life objectives. By making financial commitments and prioritizing financial freedom, you can create a cohesive strategy to improve your financial situation and work toward a more secure and fulfilling future.

To conclude, let's say you have a significant amount of credit card debt that you want to pay off. To make a financial commitment, you decide to allocate a specific portion of your monthly income to pay down the debt systematically. You create a debt repayment plan, cut back on unnecessary expenses, and commit to using any extra money, like bonuses, to accelerate your debt payments. This financial commitment involves consistent efforts and discipline to reduce your debt and eventually become debt-free.

Imagine you have a long-term vision of achieving financial freedom, which, to you, means having enough passive income to cover your living expenses and enjoy life without being dependent on a traditional job. You make financial freedom a priority by investing in various income-generating assets, such as stocks, real estate, or a business, with the goal of building a diversified portfolio that generates passive income over time. You actively manage your investments, focus on increasing your earning potential, and make strategic life decisions that align with your financial independence goal. Your financial freedom priority influences choices like living within your means, avoiding excessive debt, and seeking opportunities to grow your wealth and achieve financial autonomy in the future.

In this example, the financial commitment is the specific action taken to pay off credit card debt, while the financial freedom priority shapes long-term decisions and goals related to building wealth and achieving financial independence. Both aspects are essential for a sound financial strategy, as financial commitments help address immediate financial challenges, while prioritizing financial freedom provides a broader vision for long-term financial security and prosperity.

I recommend reading 'Setting Priorities So You Can Achieve Goals That Matter' on wishingwellcoach.com. It will help you to further understand the value of priorities.

It's amazing what we can achieve and accomplish once we align our priorities and set our mindsets to the goal we care about.

This leads us to the core subject in the book, the biggest struggle we all have: our mindset.

CHAPTER 6

LESSON #4: YOUR MINDSET IS YOUR SUCCESS

How to strengthen it

What is the potential of any human being? Look around you, and you will find many people who have accomplished great things in life. We can see the enormous potential of humans to achieve the impossible. The impossible is possible if we have the right mindset.

Look at extreme sports as an example. What do you think? Do our results reflect our true potential? What people can achieve is amazing, but what people will not do is disappointing. And it's not because we are not capable; it is the fear of doing or even trying that paralyzes most of us.

One remarkable example of a human achieving something considered impossible is the story of Roger Bannister. On May 6, 1954, Bannister, a British middle-distance runner, became the first person in history to run a mile in under four minutes. At that time, breaking the four-minute barrier was believed to be physically impossible for the human body.

Bannister's achievement was not only a testament to his physical abilities but also a demonstration of the power of the human mind and determination. His record-breaking run inspired countless athletes around the world to push their limits and strive for greatness.

Bannister's accomplishment serves as a powerful reminder that with unwavering belief, relentless effort, and a refusal to accept limitations, we can overcome seemingly any challenges and achieve what was once considered impossible. It's a testament to the incredible potential within each of us to defy expectations and make history.

The point is that we have the potential to achieve so much more in life, and yet we do not follow through. We do not pursue our goals simply because we have limiting mindsets.

By the end of this chapter, you will have learned the strategies you need to train your mindset to become more powerful and stronger so that you can get what you want. You will come to the realization that the mind is a muscle, and just like any other muscle we have in our body, requires an immense amount of training and practice to master.

Athletes are known for their mental toughness and ability to overcome obstacles, which is why adopting an athlete's mindset can be beneficial in all areas of life. Athletes approach challenges with a growth mindset, meaning that they see setbacks as opportunities to learn and grow. They also set specific, measurable goals and develop a plan to achieve them.

With a strong work ethic and unwavering determination, athletes push past their limits to achieve success.

So, let's talk about the athlete's disciplined mindset. You might be thinking, 'I'm not an athlete. Why do I need an athlete's mindset?' Well, let me tell you, having an athlete's mindset can benefit anyone regardless of whether they participate in sports or not. An athlete's mindset is all about approaching challenges with a positive attitude, staying motivated, and setting goals to achieve success. It's about pushing yourself to reach your full potential and never giving up, even when things get tough. It is so important for everyone to adopt this mindset because it can help us succeed in all areas of our lives.

So, what again is an athlete's mindset? An athlete's mindset is a way of thinking that allows us to approach challenges with a positive attitude, focus on goals, and persevere through adversity.

Having an athlete's mindset can lead to increased motivation, allowing us to push ourselves harder and achieve more than we thought possible. Resilience is another benefit of adopting an athlete's mindset. Athletes often face setbacks and challenges, but they learn to bounce back and keep moving forward. This skill can be applied in all areas of life, as we said before, and not just in sports. Goal-setting skills are also improved with an athlete's mindset. Athletes set clear and measurable goals for themselves, which helps them stay focused and motivated. We can apply the same goal-setting techniques to our personal and professional lives.

Now, how to develop an athlete's mindset.

To develop an athlete's mindset, it is important to start with setting clear and specific goals. This means breaking down larger goals into smaller, achievable milestones. Doing this allows you to create a roadmap for success that will keep you motivated and focused.

Visualization is another powerful tool for developing an athlete's mindset. Studies show that this technique has yielded positive results. Take time each day to visualize yourself achieving your goals and performing at your best. This will help you stay motivated and focused on your goals. It's important to be aware of our own weaknesses and strengths to be able to develop the athlete's mindset.

YOUR CURRENT SITUATION IS NOT YOUR FINAL GOAL

When you are facing a difficulty, start by asking yourself a question. What does the situation mean to you? When you do that, you are really telling yourself that you are in control of your perspective if not the situation. You realize that you have a choice. This way, your perspective becomes your power. You can let the situation either control you or shape you by making a certain choice. When you define a particular situation and give it a meaning (what does it mean to you and only you?), you allow yourself to control how it feels, and by doing that, you control the actions you take, which will, in turn, produce the results that you want.

Everything you face in life starts with perspective—the meaning you give to a situation. Life is about how you respond, the meaning to what happened to you, the perspective of what happened to you. How you represent the outer world within determines your mindset.

The athlete's mentality we just explained is a powerful tool that determines your mindset and helps you take control of your situation.

If you have your vision clear, you can keep building the certainty inside of you and keep the momentum going in any situation. You execute more and keep practicing. Repetition is an essential skill, I've heard from other coaches, that leads to a successful mindset.

If you have done something many times with the needed energy, you are going to master it, no doubt.

Another helpful way for our mindsets to be strengthened is to understand the difference between the growth mindset and the fixed mindset. Mindset, in this way, is defined based on the way you approach obstacles. People who have a growth mindset believe that even if they struggle with certain skills, they can overcome them by improving over time.

The opposite of that is having a fixed mindset, which basically refers to zero adaptability or change, just remaining with the status quo. Having a growth mindset can have real benefits. It helps you reframe your approach to obstacles and challenges and helps you stay committed to improving your skills. And this is where you start responding to any situation or any circumstances you are facing positively. The theory of growth mindset isn't new. It came out of research by a Stanford psychologist, Carol Dweck.

Dweck's research focused on kids, but the concept applies to all of us. The growth mindset is a belief system that all of us can learn if we are willing to improve. Ultimately, we can't control the things that happen to us, but with no doubt, we can control the way we respond. Carol Dweck studies human motivation. She spends her days diving into why people succeed or don't and what's within our control to foster success. Her theory of the two mindsets and the difference they make in outcomes is incredibly powerful.

Your view of yourself can determine everything. If you believe that your qualities are unchangeable, i.e., have a fixed mindset, you will want to prove yourself correct over and over rather than learn from your mistakes. As established earlier, everything we talk about is driven by our state of mind. When we face any challenge or obstacle in our daily lives, the number one factor that determines the way we act is our state of mind at that point in time. If we are in a positive state of mind, our response would probably be in a positive manner. However, if we were in a negative state of mind, we would for sure overreact in a negative way even when faced with a minor challenge.

THE TCDF MINDSET

Here, I would like to introduce a framework that I use to build and strengthen the mindset I need to overcome challenges during my journey and stay focused on my goals. The framework that I developed is called the TCDF mindset framework.

The first perspective is the **trust mindset**. This part of your mindset is driven by trusting yourself, your competencies, experiences, and skills. With this level of trust, you move toward the second perspective.

The second perspective is the **committed mindset**. This part of mindset is driven by your principles and boundaries. You stay committed and don't accept quitting. Staying committed and not quitting is a boundary that you should never cross, no matter what. Having such boundaries leads you to the third perspective.

This is the **do-it mindset**. This part of the mindset is driven by having certainty in the results of your actions, as it enables your body and mind to produce the right emotions for you to act, i.e., the do it mentality.

The fourth perspective is the **fighter mindset**, where you will follow through with your action no matter what. It drives your discipline and focus and enables you to stay on the path. In addition, being a fighter ensures that you never allow anything (a negative thought or any other obstacle) to stand between you and what you want to achieve.

Starting from your inner self (the trust mindset), driven by your higher degree of commitment, your principles, and boundaries (the committed mindset), allows you to take the

The TCDF Mindset Framework

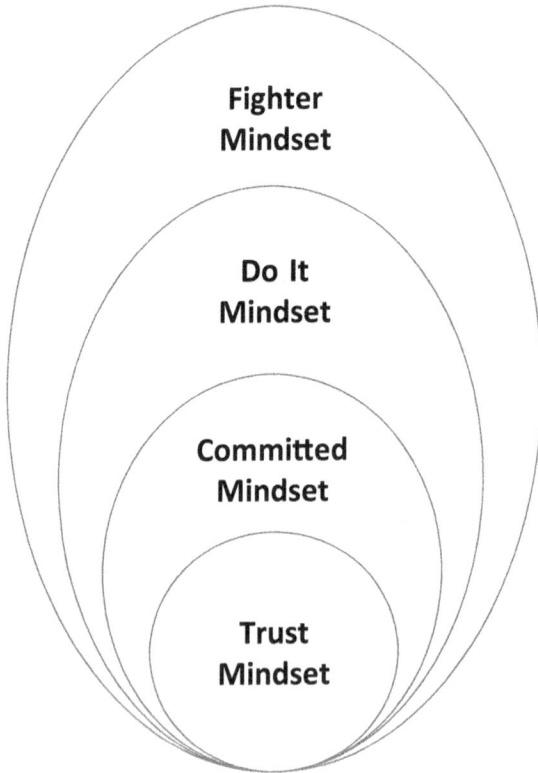

Fighter
Mindset

Do It
Mindset

Committed
Mindset

Trust
Mindset

needed action (the do it mindset), supported by your belief and sense to follow through your actions (the fighter mindset).

Drawing this framework will build the needed cycle in your mind for every single action you take in your life.

BELIEFS ARE POWERFUL

What is a belief? A belief is a mental attitude or conviction that something is true, real, or valid, regardless of whether there is evidence to support it. Beliefs shape our perceptions, thoughts, and behaviors, influencing how we interpret the world around us and make decisions. Beliefs can be based on personal experiences, cultural influences, religious teachings, social interactions, and more.

A belief is a sense of certainty about the meaning of something. The right belief combined with certainty means success. Knowledge alone is not the real power; the real power comes from combining the knowledge you have with execution, in which you end up building new experiences and new learnings. Remember, you are compounding your value!

There are different levels to our beliefs based on their certainty or strength. The first level, weak belief, can be merely opinion and comes with no references (not enough evidence to support it).

The second level, moderate belief, can be a belief with references, but it can be changed or completely removed. We are open to reevaluating this belief based on new information.

The third level, strong belief, is a belief that is a conviction with deeper references. This is the most difficult to change, sometimes even impossible to change. We hold this belief with a high degree of certainty and may be resistant to changing our stance, even when confronted with conflicting evidence.

HOW TO IDENTIFY YOUR NEGATIVE BELIEFS

Look at a certain belief as a house with foundations. The house represents a specific belief, and the foundations are different references, experiences, comments you've heard from others, and ultimately, the evidence that exists in your mind to support it. All these collectively build that specific belief in your mind. The way that we create doubt about our beliefs is by questioning them. So, we must start questioning those beliefs. Are they true? How much are we really committing to them? Is there conflicting evidence? Are the beliefs merely opinions? Do they remain beliefs with references? If those references are removed or even changed, are they still convictions?

Regularly questioning our beliefs is key to building that positive mindset and eliminating negative beliefs. The only way to keep a belief, positive or negative, is to not question it at all, and that's why this particular belief becomes your reality.

HOW TO ELIMINATE A NEGATIVE BELIEF

Step 1: Identify an old negative belief. Reject it and consider it to be untrue or invalid.

Step 2: Identify the consequences of that belief. What did this belief keep you from doing or trying? What has it cost you so far in life?

Step 3: Create your new positive belief. This is the opposite of your identified negative belief. Write it down and acknowledge it.

Step 4: Own how this new belief will change your life. With this new belief, how much more fulfillment would you have? Really acknowledge and appreciate the benefits of adopting this new positive belief in your life.

Step 5: Keep evaluating once you have adopted the new positive belief. Life evolves, so do we.

Belief is a system that is built around us. As we explained earlier, it comes from us, our interaction with others, statements we've heard from others, and our experiences. The beauty is that your mind does not know the difference between something you imagine or did in reality.

The brain works as a protector more than anything else; our brains are created to protect us. So, they are in survival mode rather than thriving mode. We need to understand this concept, and from there, we can adapt and understand how to train the brain as a muscle.

The world that protects you limits you. It protects you from fear; fear of failure, fear of others, and fear of new challenges. And this world becomes your belief system, your reality, a world that limits you. We want to question these beliefs. Discover these self-limiting beliefs, eliminate them, and replace them with new positive beliefs that empower you.

We must realize that the most sophisticated pharmacy in the universe is in our brains. It is called the hypothalamus, and it produces chemicals on demand, consistent with the way we think, feel, and perceive things that happen to us.

So, if you feel brave, you will produce a chemical called INTERLEUKIN 2 (pronounced *enterlockinto*). Your body produces it in the right quantity and sends it to the right place at the right time. When you feel calm, you produce your own Valium. When you are happy, you produce other different types of chemicals. The bottom line here is that your body can heal itself, provided you are thinking the right way. Thinking the wrong way just produces alternative results. Always focus on the positive, be brave, be happy, be healthy, so you can always be in control of your state of mind.

A great example of someone with an athlete's mindset would be none other than Michael Jordan. For the few who don't know him, he's considered one of the GOATs in the basketball game. A renowned NBA player, he was my idol when I grew up. I started watching sports at a very young age, and he was widely regarded as one of the greatest basketball players of all time. His relentless work ethic and determination to succeed are key components of his athlete's mindset. Even when he faced setbacks and failures, and he faced a lot of them, he continued to push himself to be better to achieve greatness.

In conclusion, adopting an athlete's mindset can have a profound impact on your life. By approaching challenges with a positive attitude, setting goals, visualizing success, and staying focused, you can increase your motivation, resilience, and goal-setting skills. People who adopt an athlete's mindset achieve great success in both their personal and professional lives. By embracing this mindset, you can take ownership of your life and become the best version of yourself.

In my first Iron Man race, I surpassed my own beliefs and those of others. What helped me is the thirty-minute to one-hour exercise sessions I started in 2016, and I've stayed disciplined to date. There have been times that I didn't feel like exercising, but I am proud that I have stuck to these sessions at least eighty-five percent of the time. Of course, when I decided to start training for Iron Man in September 2019, it was a completely different type of training. Nonetheless, my daily sessions made it easier, or you could say, made me better and ready to go through such different and specialized training.

On race day, my objective was very clear. I simply wanted to finish, and this is exactly what I did; I had believed this from the start. I wanted to evaluate myself during the race. The Iron Man race, 70.3 miles, consists of a 1.9-kilometer swim, 90km cycling, and 21.1km run. I can proudly say that I finished the course against all odds in six hours and forty-six minutes with no injury. Thank you, God.

In terms of the lessons learned, the first is that preparation is the work. No one knows that you are ready except yourself. I didn't mention that I registered for the race in March 2019, but I didn't participate immediately because I knew I was not ready. But in March 2022, I believed in the work I had put in, and I was completely confident I would finish the course. Guess what? I surprised myself and especially my wife.

Second, other key factors that made me finish that race as planned were consistency and discipline, enjoying the journey, and willingness to endure pain.

One question comes to mind: 'Is falling short of our expectations considered failure?' Not at all. When we fall short, we must evaluate the reasons we fell short. By doing so, we come to understand the things that went wrong, and from that we learn and gain experiences. This is how we build our confidence. Our priorities can shift, regardless, and this is why we must be adaptable.

Finally, I realized that the measure of my success was not the race results but the journey I went through, the targets that I set for myself, the improvements, and the pain. Triathlon training pushes you to the limits both physically and mentally, both while preparing and on the race day itself. However, the gratitude for the opportunity to be able to pursue such a dream is considered a success.

CONDITIONS FOR SUCCESS

Training your mind to make it more powerful involves developing a positive and growth-oriented outlook on life. Here are some strategies to help you achieve this:

1. **Adapt a growth mindset:** Embrace the belief that your abilities and intelligence can be developed through dedication and hard work. See challenges as opportunities to learn and improve rather than threats to your self-esteem.
2. **Set clear goals:** Define specific and realistic goals for yourself. Break them down into smaller, manageable steps, and celebrate your achievements along the way. This will keep you motivated and focused on your progress.
3. **Practice self-awareness:** Pay attention to your thoughts and emotions. Identify any negative or limiting beliefs you may have and work on changing them into positive and empowering ones.
4. **Challenge negative thinking:** Whenever you catch yourself engaging in negative self-talk or limiting thoughts,

challenge them with evidence to the contrary. Replace them with positive affirmations and constructive thoughts.

5. **Embrace failure as a learning opportunity:** Instead of fearing failure, view it as a chance to learn and grow. Analyze what went wrong, extract the lessons, and use that knowledge to improve in the future.

6. **Surround yourself with positivity:** Associate with people who uplift and support you. Avoid toxic relationships and negative environments that can drag you down.

7. **Practice gratitude:** Regularly acknowledge and appreciate the good things in your life. Gratitude can help shift your focus from what you lack to what you have, promoting a more positive mindset.

8. **Develop resilience:** Life is filled with challenges, setbacks, and obstacles. Cultivate resilience by viewing difficulties as temporary and finding ways to bounce back stronger after adversity.

9. **Engage in continuous learning:** Stimulate your mind by learning new things regularly. Read books, take courses, attend workshops, and engage in activities that expand your knowledge and skills.

10. **Visualize success:** Use visualization techniques to imagine yourself achieving your goals and living the life you desire. Visualization can enhance your confidence and motivation to make it a reality.

11. **Practice mindfulness and meditation:** Mindfulness can help you become more aware of your thoughts and emotions, allowing you to respond to situations in a more thoughtful and intentional manner.

12. **Take care of your physical health:** A healthy body supports a healthy mind. Exercise regularly, eat nutritious food, get enough sleep, and manage stress effectively.

Remember that training your mind and developing a positive mindset is an ongoing process. Be patient with yourself, and don't expect overnight changes. Consistent effort and practice will lead to a more powerful and positive mindset over time.

Always remember that you must:

1. Keep questioning all your beliefs.
2. Decide, act, and apply changes when needed.
3. Keep taking action until you find what you want. Imagine you're still dealing with your newborn baby, trying to teach him to walk. You will simply keep encouraging him to keep trying until he walks. By applying the same mindset to how you approach every situation, you continue acting until you succeed.
4. Keep progressing at your own pace. This is very important.
5. Acknowledge and appreciate all the blessings in your life.

Now, this leads deeper into the implications of *not* taking action. We must really understand how this is detrimental to who we become. In the next chapter, we will learn how to make our decisions and choices in life and act. But first, we need to refuel ourselves by changing our beliefs. By changing our beliefs, we can develop the right mindset.

CHAPTER 7

LESSON #5:
NOT TAKING ACTION IS
AN ACTION BY ITSELF

You must believe that the implications of not taking action are disastrous

I always ask myself why most of us, including me, end up not taking the action that matters to our lives. This can be in our careers, in dealing with a certain situation, or in dealing with our significant other or with our kids. It's something we face in every aspect of our lives. How many times do we feel lost? And what are the whys? What is stopping us from taking action?

It's easy to get stuck in situations and feel like we are not making progress towards our goals—but the truth is, if we don't take action, we will never achieve the things we want in life.

THE CAUSE OF INACTION

In this chapter, we will discuss something, a topic that affects us all, and that is taking action in life. We will also explore the consequences of not taking action, including regret, missed opportunities, and stagnation. We will discuss how fear can hold us back from taking action and offer strategies for us to overcome it.

By the end of this chapter, I hope you will be inspired to make positive changes in your life and take action toward achieving your goals. My message, a statement that you'll see across this chapter, is what could have been if action was taken. You will come to realize that by not taking action in your life, you already took the most important action that has shaped your life. You will also come to realize that if you don't change this behavior, your life will continue in the same pattern.

The cost of not taking action is detrimental. Our emphasis on the cost here, of course, is not monetary. Rather, it is the opportunities, the experiences that we lose from not taking action, the limited version of a person we become as opposed to the person we are able to become. In this chapter, you will learn how to make decisions, take action, and be decisive.

A few concepts that I share with you will provide a context for what we lose out on for not taking action.

REGRET

Regret is a powerful emotion that can haunt us for years, even decades. It is the feeling of wishing we had done something differently, taken a chance, or pursued a dream. When it comes to not taking action in life, regret is often the result.

We look back on missed opportunities and wonder what could have been. The negative impact of regret can be profound. It can lead to depression, anxiety, and a sense of hopelessness. We may feel like we've wasted our lives or that we are stuck in a situation we believe we can't change. Regret can also rob us of our motivation and make it difficult to move forward.

MISSED OPPORTUNITIES

Missed opportunities are a common result of not taking action in life. They can lead to disappointment and frustration, leaving us wondering what could have been. For example, imagine someone who always wanted to start their own business, but never took the first step. Years down the line, they see a successful entrepreneur who started their business around the same time they had their own idea. This missed opportunity can be a painful reminder of what could have been. Another example is when someone wants to pursue a romantic interest, but never takes the chance to express their feelings. They may later find out that the person they were interested in felt the same way. But by then, it is too late. This missed opportunity can leave them with a sense of regret and longing for what could have been.

STAGNATION

Stagnation is a state of being stuck in one place without any progress or growth. When we don't take action in life, we risk falling into this trap. We might feel comfortable in our current situation, but it can become suffocating and draining over time. This lack of personal growth can have negative effects on our mental and emotional wellbeing. Imagine someone who has been working the same job for years without any opportunities for advancement. They might feel bored, unfulfilled, and unmotivated. They might start to question their purpose in life and feel like they are not making any meaningful contributions to society. This can lead to feelings of depression, anxiety, and low self-esteem. But the good news is, it's never too late to break out of this cycle. We can start to build momentum and create positive change in our lives by taking small steps toward our goals. Whether it's learning a new skill, pursuing a passion, or taking a risk, every action we take can help us grow and evolve as individuals.

FEAR

Fear is a powerful emotion that can prevent us from taking action in our lives. Whether it's fear of failure, rejection, or the unknown, it can be paralyzing and keep us stuck in a place. For example, someone who is afraid of failing may never pursue their dreams or take risks because they are too afraid of not succeeding. It is important to acknowledge our fears and understand where they come from. Once we do this, we can begin to develop strategies for overcoming them. One technique is to break down our goals into smaller, more manageable steps, tasks, and milestones. This can help us feel less overwhelmed and more confident in our ability to succeed. Another strategy is to reframe our thoughts and focus on the positive outcomes that could result from taking action. By doing so, we can shift our mindset from one of fear to one of possibility and opportunity.

DOES SAFETY REALLY MEAN SAFE?

I would like to answer this question by introducing a concept used in the fundamentals of behavioral finance by investment professionals, a concept called loss aversion bias. What is loss aversion bias? Loss aversion is the tendency to avoid losses over achieving equivalent gains. Broadly speaking, people feel pain from losses much more acutely than pleasure from gains of the same size. Loss aversion bias typically shows up in financial decisions. People often need an extra and sometimes significant incentive to take financial risks that might result in a loss. Nobel Prize-winning economist Daniel Kahneman says that 'the response to losses is stronger than the response to corresponding gains'. This is his definition of loss aversion. 'Losses loom larger than gains' implies that people, by nature, are aversive to losses and tend to avoid them. Daniel Kahneman illustrated how this plays out in a simple experiment he did with his students. He told them that if a flipped coin landed on tails, they would lose $10. Then he asked them how much they would need him to stake for the coin flip to be worth the risk of losing the $10.

The answer was $50, more than $20. Why does this matter?

Loss aversion means that clients avoid risk, leading to overly conservative portfolios that do not deliver the returns they need to achieve their goals. It can push clients to sell during a stock market downturn simply because they want to avoid losses. Conversely, loss aversion can lead clients to hold on to investments that have declined in value to avoid realizing the loss in their portfolio, even when selling is the prudent decision. Inevitably, an investor who suffers from loss aversion bias will not take action and sell his investments even though it is a prudent one. They have a fear of the current reality of losses. Instead, the investor is under the illusion that his investments will rise in value, which, in fact, is the opposite, and they'll end up losing even more.

Now, if you observe how we act in our normal lives, you'll be surprised that most of us are playing the loss aversion bias game without even realizing it, and that's exactly what you want to avoid. Avoid directing your thoughts from a safety standpoint as this, more probably than not, will lead you to not take the necessary actions in your life when needed.

If you want to manage your life, don't ask yourself, 'What do I need to do?'. Rather, you must know what you really want by asking yourself three questions.

1. What is the outcome you are seeking?
2. What is your purpose? Why do you want it?
3. What is your action plan?

It is easy to make decisions when you are clear on what you want. Clarity is your main source of power.

There is a major difference between a leader and a follower. Why are there people who live their dream while the rest don't? One reason here: The people who live their dreams take massive action about their lives. We all know that taking action comes from making decisions. When it comes to decisions, there are no right or wrong ones.

We must take proactive action because circumstances change, and we must do what we can to keep in control of our lives.

Take a moment and visualize this cycle. Top coaches recommend a technique that says success results from good decision judgment, which results from experience. Meanwhile, the experience results from bad decisions and judgment. Think about it for a minute. If this is true, what does success and/or failure really mean? In my opinion, they mean nothing more than that they are part of the decision-making we go through in our daily lives. That's it! They are only results and should not be used as a measure of any kind. More specifically, they are not meant to define us! You get the point, right? I can't agree more.

The first fact is that there are no right or wrong decisions. A real decision is a decision that is driven by your commitment, keeps you focused on what matters to you, sets your expectations, and allows you to live up to them.

The second fact is that you must continue evaluating your life. If you don't like something in it, simply change it. Change can only happen when you believe that you have the capacity to choose. Create new patterns in your life.

The third fact is that too many options or fears hold us back from making decisions.

The fourth fact is that a decision needs to be made from a positive state. Having a positive state has been explained extensively in the previous chapter.

SMALL STEPS

In conclusion, we have explored the negative impact of not taking action in life. We discussed how regret can haunt us and how missed opportunities can lead to disappointments and frustration. We also explored how stagnation can be detrimental to our wellbeing and how fear can hold us back. It's clear that taking action in life is crucial for personal growth and fulfillment, but it's not enough to simply recognize the importance of taking action. We must actively make changes in our lives to achieve our goals and live a fulfilling life. This may require stepping out of our comfort zones, facing our fears, and embracing new opportunities. Remember, every small step counts toward progress and growth.

For this to work, first, you need to establish a positive mindset for yourself. I'm going to share lessons that are very important for you to establish the right mindset to execute.

- Lesson #1: Your focus determines your feeling, so it's always your choice what you focus on. This is where you are going to spend your energy and concentration, so your focus is very important.

- Lesson #2: Give proper meaning to the things that happen to you, as this will influence the decisions you make. Things will happen to you. You are part of life, and life is always going to come to you. What is under your control is that you give these actions your own meaning. Let them have a meaning to your purpose, so you are able to make decision.

- Lesson #3: The survival state is not conducive enough to make you succeed. The quality of your life is driven by the quality of your decisions. Think for a moment. What are the types of decisions you've made so far that have shaped your present? Always keep in mind the power of decision-making. By making decisions more often, it becomes a habit. As we said before, there are no wrong and right decisions. Avoid thinking about the perfect ones. They do not exist. Information evolves over time, and if you wait too long, wanting to know more before making a decision, you will realize the opportunity is gone. Circumstances keep changing. The decision that you took yesterday may face different circumstances tomorrow or next week, but you can't hold your decision waiting for the circumstances, so make it a habit and make decisions more often. Learn from your decisions. Decision-making is not static. It is a continuous process that keeps you learning.

- Lesson #4: If you don't make a decision, you do nothing. In this case, you will remain below the radar and avoid stress, at least in the short term. But you will learn nothing. You will have no experience or confidence. You will always feel fearful about failing or fearful about something else. Trust me, when you learn something new, you become a different person and create a different life, and the meanings that you give to life will be totally different.

- ○ Be disciplined and stay committed to your decisions. However, be flexible in your approach.
- ○ Enjoy making these decisions. Enjoy the power of learning, the knowledge, and the confidence that comes from making those decisions.
- Lesson #5: When making decisions, use your best judgment and do what feels right to you. Research, review your skills, and then observe your environment. All these internal and external assessments are necessary.

DO NOTHING, HAVE NOTHING, BE NOTHING

We need to start building the habit of making decisions as part of our lives. The points below are from a Tony Robbins workshop I attended. He explained four ways to create a new habit, and I would like to share the same with you here.

First, begin with habit-stacking. Simply stack one habit on top of another, so after a while, you end up doing both without even thinking about them. For example, if you wake up and make your tea in the morning the first time, the second time, the third time, you will realize that it will soon become a habit.

Second, start small, even if it's a big decision. Don't get over-whelmed. Just start small. If you go to the gym, you can't start lifting big weights from the start. You need to start with light weights and go up gradually while you strengthen your muscles. This is the same concept we need to apply when it comes to our decision-making muscles.

Third, expand it in a small way. This is where you build momentum. You must try and get yourself into an energized state, a positive mindset when making decisions.

Finally, and very simply, you must keep repeating your newly formed habit consistently.

The next topic to discuss is how to communicate and master the art of communication. Let's go.

CHAPTER 8

LESSON #6:
HOW TO COMMUNICATE

The way that you influence others is
determined by the way you communicate!

You can understand the momentum we are building, starting from having the clarity of who you are, your purpose, what you want, your priorities, and your expectations. This is the mindset you must have to have full control over every situation in your life.

When you see someone who communicates well, and you feel impressed by them, what is the reason? It may be a combination of factors, their level of preparation on the topic, the number of times they have done it, their confidence level, etc. All these factors, however, are built around one basic principle—Having The Right Mindset. The right mindset requires confidence, and one of the effective ways to build your confidence is by becoming an effective communicator.

By the end of this chapter, you will learn the invisible things effective communicators do. You will learn the patterns you must adopt and the behavioral changes you must make to become more influential and more engaging while communicating.

BASICS OF HOW TO COMMUNICATE

Let's start first by defining communication. Communication is defined as the ability to convey or share ideas and feelings effectively. Several experts agree that communication skills include:

1. Conveying messages without misinterpretating or misleading others.
2. Effectively communicating with a wide range of people from all parts of life.
3. Navigating from casual or informal communication to formal communication.
4. Showing language mastery and demand.

Did you know that communication is the number one soft skill among all other skills? It is an essential skill for achieving success in all aspects of life, so why not master it?

The two communication styles are:

- Verbal, including written communication.
- Non-verbal, which is your body language, eye contact, posture, breathing, emotions, and control while speaking.

The focus of this chapter is on oral and non-verbal ways of communication.

Now, what are the necessary skills needed to improve our communication skills?

Take work as an example. One of the benefits of effective communication in the workplace is improved productivity. The evidence shows that our productivity increases when we communicate effectively. Another benefit is increased morale and higher employee satisfaction.

The main reason is clarity. When we communicate effectively, we tend to be clear with our intentions, which results in high employee satisfaction and increased morale. There is also greater trust in management. There is also stronger teamwork, which leads to higher employee engagement.

This results in clear responsibilities, accountability, reporting lines, and work structure. Then this leads to stronger teamwork and high employee engagement.

KEY ELEMENTS FOR EFFECTIVE COMMUNICATION

1. **Active listening:** How did it feel when you talked to someone and that someone was not listening? The answer is frustrating, isn't it? Listening is fifty percent or even more of the communication process.
2. **Oral communication:** When you speak, you must be clear and concise, with no misinterpretations. We will realize later in this chapter that speaking is a set of behaviors that we can always modify or even improve.
3. **Respect:** Respect is one of the fundamentals of successful communication. Being respectful is all about letting

others speak and knowing when to initiate conversation or respond.

4. **Confidence:** Confidence is a character trait that shows you are sure about your words, actions, and decisions, and that is something people respond to positively.

5. **Clarity:** It involves structuring your thoughts logically and having the right words to convey them as effectively as possible.

6. **Being honest:** This is a must-have character trait in all communication. You have to speak your heart and be transparent at all times.

7. **Being friendly and approachable:** This encourages open lines of communication.

And lastly, give and accept constructive feedback. To give constructive feedback, you must have listened effectively to the speaker and respected their opinion and the process. This works vice versa, of course.

Now, imagine this. If you are confident, honest, clear, and friendly, what value are you reflecting in your communication? How much more influential will you be as a human being? What would be your impact?

What you say at the beginning of any presentation can be powerful. It has been proven by many expert speakers that if we start our presentation by sharing a story and linking it to the topic, we will have increased impact and more influence on the audience. You will be able to create the required engagement with them.

PUBLIC SPEAKING STINT

My first public speaking was in 2011.

In 2010, I led the risk advisory service line in Ernst & Young, Muscat. We submitted a proposal related to internal audit and risk management work to the government for all the Ministries and the State Audit Institution of the Sultanate of Oman. This proposal was the largest in our advisory service line from the revenue and project size perspective.

After several presentations and assessments done by the government, we won the engagement and the plan was to immediately prepare for a public event where we would thank the government officials, present the scope of work, and conduct a small workshop with the internal audit teams of all the Ministries and the State Audit Institution to set and manage expectations. The event was broadcast on TV, the Minister of Finance was the guest of honor, and two other ministers attended the event.

So, how did I prepare for such an event and how did it go? This was my first public speaking event, and I can assure you that public speaking is totally different than conducting presentations, even though presentation skills are necessary to succeed in public speaking.

Public speaking requires special skills. You can say to yourself that there is no doubt that there was a huge team behind me that helped prepare for the event, being part of Ernst & Young, which is true, but they only helped me prepare for the event. There was no help related to the public speaking part. I had to be fully dependent on myself, and no one could offer me help.

A quote that I would like to mention here, which I believe is completely true, is that, 'At the time of pressure, we don't rise to the occasion, we fall to our level of preparation'. This quote has been attributed to Navy SEALs and a few other notable people.

As a person, I have my own morning routine. I wake up early in the morning to pray the dawn prayer, and then I play tennis for one hour before I go to the office. On the morning of the event, I followed my routine, and I added a small jog on the beach after my tennis session. Doing this helped me to manage my emotions, calm my nerves, and feed my body with positive thoughts and energy. During this time, I spoke to myself continuously in preparation for this big day. The night before, I had written the speech on a piece of paper. When the event started, I put the paper on the stand in front of me and started talking (without reading it, of course, to establish the necessary eye contact and get the audience engaged).

I ignored the TV cameras and the presence of the ministers, keeping my focus on the greater audience, which was around two hundred individuals. I kept myself within what I wrote, at least for the first few minutes of the event. When I finished, and others presented their part, the ministers and Ernst & Young top management representatives left the event, and then I took over and continued with the planned workshop for all participants for three hours, and we were done by noon.

Was it a success? Yes, it was. Did I make a big deal out of it in my mind, especially during the last few hours leading to the event? Yes, I did. But what made me successful in managing my emotions was my morning routine. It helped me to be in a positive state from the start.

To be honest, the beginnings matter in any presentation. So, for me, that day, even with the piece of paper (don't forget it was not fancy; it was handwritten by me), the content and my preparation mattered, and the focus that I had in those first five minutes allowed me to sail through the entire event successfully.

It is completely true that not being able to communicate effectively takes away from our credibility, authority, impact, and influence.

THE ASPECTS OF EFFECTIVE COMMUNICATION

Becoming an effective communicator requires more than just technical knowledge. Soft skills play a crucial role in enhancing communication effectiveness. Here are some essential soft skills to develop:

1. **Active listening:** Pay close attention to what others are saying and demonstrate genuine interest in their thoughts

and feelings. Avoid interrupting and show empathy to better understand their perspective.

2. **Empathy:** Put yourself in others' shoes and try to understand their emotions, needs, and concerns. Empathy fosters a supportive and respectful communication environment.

3. **Verbal clarity:** Express yourself clearly and concisely. Use appropriate language, tone, and vocabulary to ensure your message is easily understood by the audience.

4. **Nonverbal communication:** Be mindful of your body language, facial expressions, and gestures. Nonverbal cues can greatly influence how your message is perceived.

5. **Emotional intelligence:** Understand and manage your emotions and recognize the emotions of others. Emotional intelligence helps you navigate sensitive or challenging conversations effectively.

6. **Conflict resolution:** Learn to address conflicts calmly and constructively. Focus on finding solutions rather than escalating the situation.

7. **Flexibility:** Be adaptable in your communication style to suit different situations and audiences. Flexibility allows you to connect with a diverse range of people.

8. **Positive attitude:** Approach communication with a positive and optimistic mindset. A positive attitude can create a more inviting and engaging conversation.

9. **Confidence:** Believe in your abilities and ideas and speak with confidence. Confidence in yourself and your message will inspire trust in your audience.

10. **Feedback receptivity:** Be open to receiving feedback from others and use it as an opportunity for growth.

Constructive criticism can help you refine your communication skills.

11. **Persuasion and influence:** Develop the ability to persuade and influence others effectively. Understand their needs and interests to present compelling arguments.

12. **Networking and relationship-building:** Cultivate meaningful connections with others through effective networking. Building strong relationships can enhance communication and collaboration.

13. **Time management:** Respect others' time and be concise in your communication. Avoid unnecessary tangents and stay focused on the key points.

14. **Conflict management:** Learn to handle disagreements and conflicts in a constructive manner, promoting understanding and resolution.

15. **Mindfulness:** Practice being present in your interactions by focusing on the conversation at hand without distractions. Mindfulness can improve your listening and responsiveness.

Developing these soft skills will not only make you an effective communicator but also help you build stronger relationships, improve teamwork, and enhance your overall interpersonal effectiveness.

CALL TO ACTION

For this to work, I want you to break down some of these essential skills in a more detailed manner. First, work on your listening skills. To become an effective listener, try and practice the following:

a) When you listen, try to focus on the speaker and give him or her your full attention.
b) Avoid your phone or any other distraction during the session.
c) Ask clarification questions, especially when you don't understand what was said.
d) It is good to paraphrase the speaker's words.

Second, work on your body language when you speak. Take videos while you're speaking, and then observe your body language in terms of eye contact with the audience, your body position, and variety and adequacy of gestures and movements.

Third, acknowledge the fact that nervousness is part of any communication, and understand what things increase the adrenaline levels in your body when approaching a presentation.

Finally, take initiative and participate in as many presentations as you can. We reach mastery level through repetition. Now, after mastering your communication skills, it is time to go to the last and final topic of the book and discuss how to navigate through obstacles.

CHAPTER 9

LESSON #7: HOW TO NAVIGATE OBSTACLES

Challenges are opportunities.
Make them your advantage!

Have you ever in your life spent a whole day without facing a single challenge or obstacle? If the answer is yes, you know me by now: Contact me, and I will give you all the sale proceeds of this book for two years. Good deal?

Imagine a life with no obstacles. How amazing that would be. The irony of the matter is that it is to the contrary. Life with no obstacles means life with no growth, no new learnings, and no new experiences, resulting in a boring life. Will you agree? It is strange how the challenges that make us think and feel negative are the same circumstances that allow us to prosper in life.

By the end of this chapter, you will be armed with the basic tools and tactics to help you navigate the obstacles you face throughout your life. The objective here is to outline a simple strategy for how to deal with obstacles and overcome them.

START WITH WHY

Life is full of obstacles, and we have two options. Option one is that we surrender ourselves to the obstacles and do nothing. Option two is that we face them as opportunities and grow. Be true to yourself and ask yourself if you are happy where you are now in life. Throughout my career, there was no single day that passed without at least one obstacle I had to deal with, whether it was related to work or a personal matter. We are a combination of our personal and professional lives, and I'm a great believer that we can't live them separately.

When I was a manager at Ernst & Young, there was a time that we worked on a huge proposal for the government. When we reached the deadline to deliver it to the tender committee, I was told that the delivery team didn't report to work that day, and the proposal copies were not sealed as required. Now, we had only two hours to make the deadline. I remember talking to my assistant, and we agreed that we needed to take owner-ship and deliver it ourselves. We took my car and searched for libraries that could bind and seal the proposal copies, a service that most libraries did not offer. We eventually found one library to do both. By the time we finished, it was thirty minutes to the deadline. We drove to the location, reaching there just in time. We delivered the proposal on time.

And you know what? After six months of evaluation, we were awarded this project, and it was the largest advisory engagement we won in 2010. Imagine that we had failed to deliver the proposal on time despite all the hard work we did to complete it. This biggest win could have been the biggest failure instead.

Having the logistics team unavailable and not getting the proposal copies ready on the day of the deadline was an obstacle. How did I overcome it? By taking ownership of the situation, staying determined, and not finger-pointing.

Obstacles vary in their degree of difficulty. They can be as simple as the example above or something very complex. Navigating through obstacles is, however, the same regardless of the level of their difficulty. It all depends on how we react and what our perspective is on the obstacle and potential solution.

Let's start by asking ourselves, 'What is an obstacle?'. There are a lot of definitions. However, in the context of our book, we will define it as anything that stands in the way of achieving our goals. It can be in the form of a problem, a person, a challenge, a distraction, etc. It can be anything.

For every obstacle you face, ask yourself the following questions:

1. What is my perspective?
2. Am I determined? And if yes, determined to do what?
3. What is my resiliency level?

Of course, the answers to these three questions will be guided by your vision and purpose in life.

We always hear that we need to take charge of things that fall under our control, and not the things that are out of our control. From the obstacles perspective, I believe this is not true. As obstacles are going to happen either way, we need to focus on our reactions and not why these obstacles happen to us. There is absolutely no doubt that we can control our reactions completely. It all depends on how determined we are.

Our emotions are an integral part of our reactions when we face obstacles, so knowing how to control them is a must to succeed in dealing with them. Acknowledging them, even if they are negative, and adapting and moving forward is critical. Keeping a positive attitude and mindset allows our brains to function in a positive way. Research suggests that our brains do not distinguish between events resulting from our imagination or reality, which means that we have the ultimate control over our brains.

Accepting that our lives are full of obstacles and that they are there for us to learn and grow helps us look at them as opportunities rather than challenges. Whether it's a difficult work project, a challenging relationship, or a personal struggle, we all face obstacles at some point in our lives. But how we navigate these obstacles can make all the difference in achieving our goals and living a fulfilling life.

Differentiating between thoughts and facts is also crucial for overcoming obstacles. As research suggests, we are hard-wired for negativity, which means that it's natural for most of us to feel negative outcomes or emotions with a greater intensity than we do positive feelings. As a result, we end up navigating life with the tension of overthinking, which affects our mental health and stress levels. Acknowledging that you are not your thoughts will allow you to take control of them. This is something called metacognition, a physiology term.

How do we act in situations related to our insecurities or fear of change? Many psychological studies suggest that authenticity, being true to yourself, is an integral part of our happiness and can boost our self-esteem in addition to lowering stress levels. Knowing your true self can be challenging, but it's worth it as it enables you to thrive, have satisfaction in your life, build better relationships with others, and establish a sense of purpose for your life. All of this will allow us to master navigating all the obstacles we come across, with no doubt.

IDENTIFYING OBSTACLES

Obstacles can be big or small, but no matter their size, they can have a significant impact on our lives. That's why it is important to identify them so we can work to overcome them.

Common obstacles people face include financial difficulties, health issues, relationship problems, and career setbacks. These obstacles can cause stress, anxiety, and even depression. By identifying them, we can start taking steps toward finding solutions and improving our lives.

MINDSET SHIFT

We often feel defeated or overwhelmed, and this can prevent us from taking action to overcome the obstacles in our path. However, we can approach obstacles as opportunities for learning and growth by shifting our mindset to a growth mindset. A growth mindset is the belief that we can develop our abilities through hard work and dedication. With a growth mindset, we see challenges as opportunities to learn and improve rather than as threats to our abilities. This mindset allows us to persevere in the face of obstacles and to view setbacks as temporary rather than permanent.

DEVELOPING RESILIENCE

Developing resilience is key to navigating obstacles in life. Resilience is the ability to bounce back from adversity and overcome challenges, and it's a skill that can be developed over time. One way to develop resilience is by practicing self-care. This means taking care of yourself physically, emotionally, and mentally. It could be as simple as taking a walk outside or spending time with loved ones. Another way to build resilience is by seeking support from others. This could mean talking to a friend or family member, joining a support group, or seeing a therapist. By building a strong support system, you will have people to turn to when you are facing tough times.

KEY ASPECTS OF MASTERING
THE SKILL OF NAVIGATING OBSTACLES

Mastering the skill of navigating obstacles involves a combination of physical, mental, and strategic approaches. Whether you're facing obstacles in a physical environment, your career, relationships, or personal growth, these principles can be applied broadly:

1. **Develop a growth mindset:** Cultivate a mindset that embraces challenges as opportunities for learning and growth. Instead of seeing obstacles as roadblocks, view them as stepping stones to becoming better and stronger.
2. **Set clear goals:** Clearly define your objectives and goals. Knowing where you want to go will help you strategize and plan your approach to overcoming obstacles.
3. **Problem-solving skills:** Enhance your ability to analyze problems and come up with creative solutions. Break complex obstacles into smaller, manageable tasks and address them one at a time.
4. **Adaptability and flexibility:** Be willing to adapt your strategies and approaches as the situation demands. Not all obstacles can be overcome with a single fixed plan.
5. **Resilience and persistence:** Develop resilience by staying committed and persistent in the face of challenges. Understand that setbacks are a natural part of the process.
6. **Learn from failure:** Embrace failure as a valuable learning experience. Analyze what went wrong, identify lessons learned, and apply those lessons to future endeavors.

7. **Time management:** Allocate your time and resources efficiently to tackle obstacles. Prioritize tasks and avoid getting bogged down by unimportant details.

8. **Seek guidance and mentorship:** Reach out to people who have successfully navigated similar obstacles. Their insights and advice can provide valuable guidance.

9. **Visualization and mental preparation:** Visualize yourself successfully overcoming obstacles. This mental rehearsal can boost your confidence and help you approach challenges with a positive mindset.

10. **Stay positive and manage stress:** Maintain a positive attitude and manage stress effectively. Negative emotions can cloud your judgment and hinder your problem-solving abilities.

11. **Networking and collaboration:** Collaborate with others who have complementary skills. Sometimes, navigating obstacles requires a team effort and diverse perspectives.

12. **Continuous learning:** Keep learning and acquiring new knowledge relevant to your goals. The more you know, the more equipped you'll be to handle different types of obstacles.

13. **Mindfulness and self-awareness:** Develop mindfulness and self-awareness to understand your emotions and reactions better. This can help you respond to obstacles in a more composed and effective manner.

14. **Celebrate small wins:** Acknowledge and celebrate the progress you make, no matter how small. It boosts your motivation and reinforces your belief in your ability to overcome obstacles.

Remember that mastering how to navigate obstacles is an ongoing process. As you encounter different challenges, you'll refine your approach and build greater confidence in your ability to overcome them.

CALL TO ACTION

When facing obstacles, it's easy to feel overwhelmed and be unsure where to start. However, taking action is crucial to overcoming these challenges. By breaking down our goals into small, manageable steps, we can make progress and build momentum toward success. Not only does taking action help us overcome obstacles, but it also builds resilience and self-confidence. Each small step we take toward our goals reinforces the belief that we are capable of achieving them. This positive mindset can carry us through even the toughest obstacles.

For this to work, and in implementing the key aspects of navigating obstacles, you must master four things in your life and be crystal-clear about them.

1. Know your purpose.
2. Maintain your values and principles.
3. Live in the moment present before you.
4. Create and respect boundaries—your boundaries.

The most prominent characteristics to navigate obstacles, as previously said, are determination and resilience. You must have your own perspective of your values and purpose. That means to give meaning to everything that happens in your life. The meaning is relative to your values and principles, your boundaries, and how you see things. It comes from your culture. It comes from the people that you've been raised with. You must have that perspective, and you need to be crystal-clear about it. And I promise you that doing so will guarantee you success.

In conclusion, navigating obstacles in life is crucial for personal growth and development. By identifying obstacles, shifting our mindset, developing resilience, and taking action, we can overcome any challenge that comes our way. Remember, obstacles are not roadblocks, but opportunities for growth. With a positive attitude and a willingness to learn, we can turn obstacles into stepping stones toward success.

CHAPTER 10

CONCLUSION

The power of choice refers to our ability to make decisions and take actions based on our purpose, values, and goals. The power of choice represents the freedom to make decisions that align with our personal beliefs and desires. It allows us to express our uniqueness and shape our lives according to our aspirations.

With the power of choice comes responsibility for the outcomes of those choices. We are accountable for the consequences of our decisions, which can motivate us to make informed and thoughtful choices. Making choices and taking actions based on personal values and goals leads to personal growth and development. Consciously choosing to challenge ourselves, learn new skills, or step out of our comfort zone enables growth.

The ability to make choices that promote emotional well-being is vital. We can choose to engage in activities that bring us happiness, manage stress, and cultivate positive relationships. The power of choice enables us to adapt to changing circumstances and adjust as needed. It allows for the exploration of different paths and the ability to pivot when necessary.

The power of choice involves the process of evaluating options, considering consequences, and making decisions. Developing effective decision-making skills can lead to better problem-solving and improved outcomes.

When we exercise the power of choice in ways that are aligned with our values and passions, we are more likely to experience a sense of fulfillment and satisfaction in our lives. Recognizing and utilizing the power of choice empowers us to take control of our lives. It encourages a proactive and empowered mindset rather than a feeling of being a passive investor.

It's important to acknowledge that while we have the power of choice, external factors and constraints can influence those choices. Socioeconomic circumstances, cultural influences, and systemic barriers can impact the range of choices available to us. Nonetheless, understanding and embracing the power of choice can empower us to navigate our lives with intention and purpose.

Remember, decision-making is not always linear; you need to adapt and personalize your approach to suit different decision-making contexts, whether they are personal, professional, or even strategic decisions within organizations.

Incorporating creativity, critical thinking, and a willingness to learn from both successes and failures is also an essential part of the art of decision-making. Ultimately, the goal is to make choices that are well-considered, aligned with your values, and likely to lead to positive outcomes.

In essence, the art of decision-making is a skill that can be mastered through practice, self-awareness, and a willingness to adapt. By combining thoughtful analysis with an understanding of personal values and a willingness to learn, you can navigate complex choices with greater confidence and success.

AUTHOR BIO

Nashat Helal is an accomplished and growth-driven financial executive with twenty-two-plus years of experience leading the finance function as well as overseeing and implementing strategic solutions to secure organizational growth.

His expertise lies in all areas of business strategy and management, company valuation, mergers & acquisitions, IPOs, fundraising (equity & debt), company transformation and turnaround, portfolio investment and management, financial and strategic planning, and corporate finance.

Nashat has worked in and served various industries, including financial services, real estate, healthcare, contracting, maritime, hospitality, retail, automotive, management consulting, auditing, education, and trade and distribution.

He holds an Executive MBA from London Business School, UK. His bachelor's degree is in marketing from Yarmouk

University, Jordan. He also holds professional certificates, such as CFA, CPA, and CMA.

He is currently the Group CFO of Balubaid Group of Companies, a diversified holding company operating in eight sectors in Saudi Arabia.

Nashat's strong drive to continuously enhance his knowledge, skills and personal qualities, his passion became helping others and making an impact. Driven by his passion, Nashat made all his choices in life that allowed him to live up to his expectations and values. A devoted husband and proud father of 3 lovely kids, he is an athlete himself, plays tennis, and test his resilience by participating in Ironman Triathlon.

GET IN TOUCH

Website: www.nashathelal.com

LinkedIn: www.LinkedIn.com/in/nashathelal

Instagram: https://Instagram/nashelal

EARLIER ROLES

- **Group CFO, Thumbay Group LLC**, *Ajman, UAE | Mar 2022 – Mar 2023.*
- **Group CEO/CFO, BinHindi Enterprises LLC**, *Dubai, UAE. | Oct 2020 – Mar 2022.*
- **CFO and Acting CEO, Gulf Navigation Holding PJSC**, *Dubai, UAE | Aug 2018 – Sep 2020.*
- **CFO, Oman International Development & Investment SAOG**, *Muscat, Oman | Jul 2013 – Aug 2018.*
- **CFO, Oman Sail LLC**, *Muscat, Oman | Jul 2011 – Jul 2013.*
- **Executive Manager, Ernst & Young LLP**, *MENA | Dec 2002 – Jul 2011.*